Administrative Assistant: Simulated Projects

Lynn Berry

Valerie Duthie

Sandy Miller

emond

Toronto, Canada
2015

DEDICATION

To our mothers who have inspired, guided, and led by example, and to our husbands who have stood silently behind us all these years as we dedicate our lives to ensuring student success.
To our families who are our tireless cheerleaders!
To all our students past and present—you inspire us to keep learning.

Emond Montgomery Publications Limited
60 Shaftesbury Avenue
Toronto ON M4T 1A3
http://www.emp.ca/highered

Printed in Canada.
Reprinted July 2019.

We acknowledge the financial support of the Government of Canada through the Canada Book Fund for our publishing activities.

Permissions have been received from Evite®, Express Scribe, Join.me, and SurveyMonkey®.

Publisher: Mike Thompson
Managing editor, development: Kelly Dickson
Director, editorial and production: Jim Lyons
Production editor: Laura Bast
Production: First Image Graphic Design
Proofreader: David Handelsman
Cover design: Tara Wells
Cover image: Stockphoto.com / Rawpixel

Library and Archives Canada Cataloguing in Publication

Berry, Lynn M., author

    Administrative assistant : simulated projects / Lynn Berry, Valerie Duthie, and Sandy Miller.

ISBN 978-1-55239-622-3 (pbk.)

    1. Office management--Problems, exercises, etc.
    2. Administrative assistants.   I. Miller, Sandy (Sandy J.), 1961-, author
    II. Duthie, Valerie, author   III. Title.

HF5547.B47 2015   651.3   C2014-907544-8

TABLE OF CONTENTS

Introduction to Berry, Duthie & Miller (BDM) . . . . **ix**

    Company Overview ix

    Overview of Workbook x

Projects

Project 1 – Domestic Travel Arrangements and Conferences **1**

    Learning Objectives 1

    Task 1 – Highlighting and Annotating 2

    Task 2 – Appointment 2

    Task 3 – Contact 2

    Task 4– Travel Budget 2

    Task 5 – Travel Authorization 3

    Task 6 – Appointment 4

    Task 7 – Tasks 4

    Task 8 – Email 4

    Task 9 – Reply to Invitation 4

    Task 10 – Photo and Biography 5

    Task 11 – Email 5

    Task 12 – Travel Itinerary 5

    Task 13 – Speech 5

    Task 14 – PowerPoint 6

    Task 15 – Email 6

    Task 16 – Appointment 6

    Task 17 – Travel Expense Claim 6

    Task 18 – Change in Travel Plans 7

    Task 19 – Travel Checklist 8

Project 2 – Mail-Outs and Surveys **9**

    Learning Objectives 9

    Task 1 – Appointment 10

    Task 2 – Task List 10

    Task 3 – Research 10

    Task 4 – Mailings – Recipient List – Database 11

    Task 5 – Mailings – Letter with Merge Fields 11

    Task 6 – Mailings – Labels with Merge Fields 11

    Task 7 – Editing a Recipient List – Database 11

Task 8 – Confirmation Letter with Merge Fields 12

Task 9 – Appointments 12

Task 10 – Flyer 12

Task 11 – Survey 13

Task 12 – SurveyMonkey 13

Project 3 – Tables, Charts, and Reports **15**

Learning Objectives 15

Task 1 – Task 16

Task 2 – Budget 16

Task 3 – Tables – Projections and Requirements 16

Task 4 – Fax 17

Task 5 – Charts 17

Task 6 – Comparison Chart 18

Task 7 – PowerPoint 18

Task 8 – Email 18

Task 9 – Report 19

Project 4 – Meetings: Informal, Formal, and External **21**

Learning Objectives 21

Task 1 – Notice of Meeting 22

Task 2 – Agenda (Informal Style) 22

Task 3 – Revising a Set of Minutes (Informal Style) 22

Task 4 – Contact 23

Task 5 – Notice (by Evite) 23

Task 6 – Agenda (Formal Style) 23

Task 7 – Minutes (Formal Style) 24

Task 8 – Revision of Minutes (Formal Style) Using Document Tracking 24

Task 9 – Taking Minutes 24

Task 10 – Highlighting and Annotating 25

Task 11 – Tasks 25

Task 12 – Request for Proposal 25

Task 13 – Notice of Meeting 26

Task 14 – Agenda (Conference or Seminar Style) 26

Task 15 – Map and Driving Directions 26

Task 16 – Interoffice Memorandum 27

Task 17 – SurveyMonkey 27

Task 18 – Online Collaboration Using Join.me 28

Project 5 – Job Search **29**

   Learning Objectives.. 29

   Task 1 – Business Card... 30

   Task 2 – Personal List of Skills Inventory 30

   Task 3 – Researching Industry 30

   Task 4 – Job Search Tracking 30

   Task 5 – Designing a Résumé 31

   Task 6 – Applying Online 31

   Task 7 – Cover Letter 31

   Task 8 – Researching Interview Questions 32

   Task 9 – Mock Interviews 32

   Task 10 – Portfolio 32

   Task 11 – Thank-You Letter 33

   Task 12 – Post-Interview 33

Project 6 – International Travel Arrangements **35**

   Learning Objectives.. 35

   Task 1 – Online Research 36

   Task 2 – Currency Exchange 36

   Task 3 – Time Zone.. 36

   Task 4 – Travel Budget 37

   Task 5 – Travel Authorization 38

   Task 6 – Appointment.. 38

   Task 7 – Contact 38

   Task 8 – Task 38

   Task 9 – Reply to Invitation 39

   Task 10 – Canadian Passport 39

   Task 11 – Travel Itinerary... 39

   Task 12 – Email 40

   Task 13 – Letter 40

   Task 14 – Memo... 40

Appendices

A Organization Chart 41

B Corporate Policies 43

C Templates 45

    Fax Cover 46

    Interoffice Memorandum 47

    Letterhead 48

    Request for Proposal 49

    Travel Authorization 52

    Travel Expense Claim 53

    Voice Message 55

D Sample Documents 57

    Action Verbs (for Résumés and Cover Letters) 58

    Agenda (Conference or Seminar Style) 59

    Agenda (Formal Style) 60

    Agenda (Informal Style) 61

    Appointment 62

    Biography 63

    Business Cards... 64

    Contact 65

    Cover Letter (Prospecting) 66

    Cover Letter (Solicited) 67

    Email 68

    Fax Cover 69

    Highlighted and Annotated Letter 70

    Interoffice Memorandum 71

    Interview Question Examples 72

    Job Application Form 73

    Job Search Tracking 75

    Letter 76

    Minutes (Formal Style) 77

    Minutes (Informal Style) 79

    Notice of Meeting 81

    Notice of Meeting (Internal) by Email 82

    Notice of Meeting (External) by Email 83

    Post-Interview Job Search Tracking 84

    Projection Table Using an Absolute Cell Reference 85

    Request for Proposal 86

    Résumé (Chronological) 89

    Résumé (Functional) 91

    Survey (Paper Format) 93

    Task... 95

    Thank-You Letter 96

    Travel Authorization 97

    Travel Expense Claim 98

    Travel Expenses Table 100

Travel Itinerary (Domestic) 101

Travel Itinerary (International) 103

Voice Message.. 105

E Procedural Guide – Background Notes and Instructions............... 107

Agendas 108

Applying Online 109

Appointments... 110

Business Cards... 111

Cover Letters 112

Document Tracking.. 113

Editing a Merge.. 114

External Meetings 115

Formal Meetings 117

Highlighting and Annotating Correspondence..................... 119

Join.me for Online Collaboration 120

Labels 125

Meetings – an Introduction 126

Minutes of Meetings... 127

Notices of Meetings 130

Notices of Meetings Using Evite 131

Personal Skills Inventory 135

Portfolio 136

Reports 137

Request for Proposal (RFP) 138

Request for Proposal Template with Explanation 139

Researching Potential Employers 142

Résumé Writing 143

Scheduling Meetings Using MS Outlook 144

Survey (Paper Format) 149

SurveyMonkey... 151

Teleconferencing 152

Transcription 154

Travel Authorization Template with Explanation 159

Travel (International) Arrangements 161

F Related Task Documents 165

Invitation Letter – Project 1 – Task 1 166

Email from President – Project 1 – Task 18.......................... 167

Interoffice Memorandum from Director of Marketing and Sales –
Project 1 – Tasks 1, 2, 3, and 10 168

Interoffice Memorandum from Director of Finance – Project 3 –
Tasks 1 and 2.. 169

Draft Budget Form – Project 3 – Task 2 170

Interoffice Memorandum from Director of Human Resources and
Administration – Project 3 – Task 3 171

Letter from Real Estate Agent – Project 3 – Task 6 173

Draft Report – Project 3 – Task 9.................................... 175

Draft Minutes (Informal Style) – Project 4 – Task 3   179

Draft Minutes (Formal Style) – Project 4 – Tasks 5 and 7.   181

Interoffice Memorandum from Director of Training –
    Project 4 – Tasks 10 to 17.   183

Draft Agenda – Project 4 – Task 14.   184

Letter of Invitation – Project 6 – Tasks 1, 4, 6, and 11   185

G Key Documents   187

INTRODUCTION TO BERRY, DUTHIE & MILLER (BDM)

Welcome to Berry, Duthie & Miller (BDM). You have just been hired to work in this exciting team environment as an administrative assistant.

Company Overview

Berry, Duthie & Miller is a medium-sized private corporation whose objective is to provide leading-edge training in the following areas:

Office Administration

Business Administration

Software Applications

Human Resources

Finance

The contact information for the company is:

820 - 360 Albert Street

Ottawa, ON K1R 7X7

info@bdm.emp.ca

www.bdm.emp.ca

613-237-9482 (telephone)

613-237-9400 (fax)

Our firm is organized into four departments, and you will be primarily responsible for providing administrative support to the four directors. In addition, you may be required to support the president and two vice-presidents.

See Appendix A for the organization chart. There is a copy on your USB key where you can enter information as the company's administrative assistant.

Overview of Workbook

The workbook is divided into projects as follows:

Project 1	Domestic Travel Arrangements and Conferences
Project 2	Mail-Outs and Surveys
Project 3	Tables, Charts, and Reports
Project 4	Meetings: Informal, Formal, and External
Project 5	Job Search
Project 6	International Travel Arrangements

Each start-to-finish project will be divided into tasks that may involve the use of MS Word®, MS Excel®, calendar software, MS PowerPoint®, and/or the Internet.

When dates are represented as 20xx, you are to use the current year.

In addition to your scheduled project work, pop tasks will be assigned that will require your immediate action. You will have to manage your time, ensuring that all tasks are completed in an efficient manner.

Your instructor will determine the tasks you will be undertaking, the method of presentation for evaluation (printed or electronically provided), and the evaluation weighting for each task.

Resources

Each task within the project may have resources identified. Always preview the resources before commencing the task.

Appendices

For you to function effectively within Berry, Duthie & Miller, the following resources are available:

A   Organization Chart

B   Corporate Policies

C   Templates

D   Sample Documents

E   **Procedural Guide – Background Notes and Instructions**

F   **Related Task Documents**

G   **Key Documents**

Your workbook includes key electronic documents: organization chart, the logo, the templates, files required for the projects, and pop tasks.

DOMESTIC TRAVEL ARRANGEMENTS AND CONFERENCES

LEARNING OBJECTIVES

- Highlighting correspondence
- Annotating correspondence
- Scheduling appointments
- Creating a contact
- Researching travel costs
- Making travel arrangements
- Preparing a travel authorization
- Creating tasks
- Drafting emails
- Drafting a letter
- Preparing a biography
- Preparing travel itineraries
- Editing a speech
- Creating a PowerPoint presentation
- Preparing a travel expense claim
- Creating a travel checklist

In this project, you will be making the necessary arrangements so that the Director of Training can attend an out-of-town conference where he will be one of the presenters.

Pop tasks will be assigned by your instructor as you make your way through this project. These are not identified in the learning objectives.

| TASK 1 | **HIGHLIGHTING AND ANNOTATING** |

RESOURCES: Appendix D – Highlighted and Annotated Letter Sample
Appendix E – Highlighting and Annotating Correspondence
Appendix F – Invitation Letter

The Director of Training has received an invitation to attend an external conference.

You are responsible for processing all incoming mail for the directors. You are now looking at the invitation letter that has arrived.

- Using a highlighter, highlight the key points to prepare the letter for the Director of Training's Inbox.
- Using a pencil, annotate the letter with the necessary notes for the director.

| TASK 2 | **APPOINTMENT** |

RESOURCES: Calendar Software
Appendix D – Appointment Sample
Appendix E – Appointment Instructions

You have checked the director's calendar, and you need to record the dates for the conference.

- Enter the appointment in the director's calendar as tentative based on the information in the conference invitation.
- Using the Internet, you will need to determine the hotel's contact information, which should be included in the appointment entry.

| TASK 3 | **CONTACT** |

RESOURCES: Calendar Software
Appendix D – Contact Sample

The director updates his contacts based on his current working relationships.

- Create a new contact for the person sending the invitation to the director.

| TASK 4 | **TRAVEL BUDGET** |

RESOURCE: Appendix B – Corporate Policies

Conduct the research necessary to prepare a travel authorization for the conference expenses. To do this, you need to determine the estimated cost of the trip, which will include flight, hotel, meals, miscellaneous expenses, conference fee, English Bay cruise, and ground transportation, both at home and at the conference location.

Flights

- The director likes to fly direct where possible and likes to book his seat in advance.
- He prefers to leave in the morning and no later than 3 p.m.
- As per corporate policy, he will be flying economy.
- He will be returning the day after the conference.
- Download the information detailing the cost and the flight schedule.

Hotel

- Use the rate provided in the invitation letter.
- As per corporate policy, he will be requiring a single room.
- Using the Internet, determine and download the contact information for the hotel.

Ground Transportation

- Using the Internet, determine if there is a hotel shuttle and if there is a cost. If not, determine how much a taxi would be from the airport to the hotel and back.
- Locally, the director will be using taxi chits to and from the airport.

Cost Chart

- Prepare a table of your costs, indicating the expense name and the amount of the expense. Provide a total estimated budget amount. You can use MS Excel or MS Word.
  - The meal per diem is $50.
  - The miscellaneous amount (tips) is $300.
  - The conference registration fee is provided in the invitation.
  - The English Bay cruise fee is provided in the invitation.
  - Calculate the hotel charge for a single room for four nights based on the rate per night provided in the invitation.
  - The flight cost is located on your download.
  - The local ground transportation is $45 each way.
  - The ground transportation at the destination is determined through your research.

TASK 5   TRAVEL AUTHORIZATION

RESOURCES: Appendix C – Travel Authorization Template
Appendix D – Travel Authorization Sample

Check with the director to ensure that he agrees with the arrangements before making the reservations. Prepare the director's travel authorization.

- He wants a $200 cash advance.
- His flight, hotel, English Bay cruise, and registration fee are covered by corporate accounts.
- His employee number is 22339.
- His cost centre is 5400.
- The account number is 3117-00, which is the convention/conference travel account.

TASK 6	**APPOINTMENT**

RESOURCES: Calendar Software
Appendix D – Appointment Sample
Appendix E – Appointment Instructions

The director has reviewed the invitation letter received in the mail that you highlighted and annotated when it came across your desk. Assume the director has requested and received permission to attend. The director has advised you that he will be attending and presenting at the conference.

- Adjust the appointment to reflect that it is now confirmed.

TASK 7	**TASKS**

RESOURCES: Calendar Software
Appendix D – Task Sample

Your role is to keep both you and the director organized. Remember that the key to organizational success is to break a project down into tasks.

- Document the required tasks to prepare for the conference based on the invitation details in the letter.

TASK 8	**EMAIL**

RESOURCE: Appendix D – Email Sample

Cheques are prepared by BDM's Finance Department. An email request must be sent to Finance. For the director to attend the conference, two cheques must be requested in accordance with the invitation:

- Request a cheque payable as directed in the invitation for the conference registration fee.
- Request a cheque payable as directed in the invitation for the English Bay cruise.

TASK 9	**REPLY TO INVITATION**

RESOURCES: Appendix C – Letterhead Template
Appendix D – Letter Sample

The director has requested a single room for four nights, and he wants to participate in the English Bay cruise.

- Draft a reply to the invitation letter on behalf of the director indicating that he will be attending and presenting.
- Indicate that he will be participating in the English Bay cruise.
- Provide the dates of the conference.
- Provide the conference name.
- Include a subject line.
- Insert a "DRAFT" watermark.
- Advise that the speech, biography, photo, and PowerPoint presentation will be sent by email as requested in the invitation.
- Enclose the two endorsed cheques required for the registration fee and English Bay cruise.

TASK 10	**PHOTO AND BIOGRAPHY**

RESOURCES: Appendix D – Biography Sample
Appendix E – Transcription Instructions
Appendix G – Biography Voice File
www.freedigitalphotos.net
www.morguefile.com

The conference coordinator has requested that the director provide a biography with a photograph to be incorporated into the conference package.

- Obtain, from the websites provided above, a professional head shot of a business person to use as your director (passport size) and save it as a JPEG file. Ensure that you do not distort the photo when sizing it.
- Paste it or insert it into a Word document at the top left of the page.
- To the right of the photo and centred, key the title "BIOGRAPHY."
- The subtitle should be the director's name.
- Transcribe the biography from the Biography Voice File.

TASK 11	**EMAIL**

RESOURCE: Appendix D – Email Sample

The conference coordinator has requested that the biography and photo be emailed to her.

- Draft an email as per the invitation letter, enclosing the biography and photo.

TASK 12	**TRAVEL ITINERARY**

RESOURCE: Appendix D – Travel Itinerary – Domestic – Sample

Prepare an itinerary for the trip ensuring that the director knows the dates and locations of the events:

- Flight times and flight numbers
- Ground transportation, locally and at travel destination
- Hotel contact information, including hotel check-in and check-out times
- English Bay cruise
- Conference
- Presentation by director (date and time)
- To be consistent, create all times in the intinerary using the 24-hour clock

TASK 13	**SPEECH**

RESOURCE: Appendix G – Draft Speech

The director requires a speech for his presentation, and he has provided you with a draft to edit into final form.

- Double space the document.
- Edit the speech by correcting the errors in spacing, formatting, grammar, and spelling. Avoid using convoluted sentences.

- Ensure the font is large enough (14 or 16 points) so it can be read from the podium.
- Use graphic lines to separate sections, indicating when to change the slides.
- Ensure you indicate on the speech where the next slide begins in the PowerPoint you will be preparing by using an icon, symbol, or the words [click] or [next slide].
- You will be using this draft to prepare a PowerPoint presentation.

TASK 14 | **POWERPOINT**

The director requires a PowerPoint presentation that aligns with the speech so he can refer to it from the podium at the conference. Create the PowerPoint slides according to the following specifications:

- The slides are paginated.
- Slide 1 contains the following details:

  Name of presenter, position, name of company, logo of company, address of company, phone number of company, website of company, and photo of director
- Slides 2+ (up to 6 slides) contain the following details:
  - A header or footer with the company name and logo on all slides except the title slide
  - A summary of the speech, which includes key points that correspond to the text

---

TASK 15 | **EMAIL**

RESOURCE: Appendix D – Email Sample

The conference coordinator requires the speech and PowerPoint presentation in advance by email.

- Prepare an email from the director to the appropriate person in the invitation letter, attaching the speech and PowerPoint presentation.

TASK 16 | **APPOINTMENT**

RESOURCES: Calendar Software
Appendix D – Appointment Sample
Appendix E – Appointment Instructions

You have now made the travel arrangements for the director, and you need to update the director's calendar.

- Include the travel times to and from the conference in the calendar.

TASK 17 | **TRAVEL EXPENSE CLAIM**

RESOURCES: Appendix C – Travel Expense Claim Template
Appendix D – Travel Authorization
Appendix D – Travel Expense Claim Sample

The director has returned from his trip. He has provided you with his receipts, and you now have to prepare his travel expense claim. The dates will match the order in which the expenses were incurred.

- Use only the following expenses, rather than those you obtained in your research, to prepare the claim.

  - Conference fee $2,500.00
  - Cruise $100.00
  - Taxi to airport $45.00 (Blue Line chit no. 13555)
  - Airfare $541.10 (Air Canada)
  - Taxi to hotel $25.00
  - Hotel $837.78
  - Meals $15.00 for lunch on flight
                            $20.00 for dinner upon arrival at hotel
                            $15.00 for dinner on flight home
  - Taxi to airport $23.00
  - Taxi from airport $45.00 (Blue Line chit no. 16454)

- Use the travel authorization to assist in finding information for the expense claim.

TASK 18

CHANGE IN TRAVEL PLANS

RESOURCES: Appendix B – Corporate Policies
Appendix F – Email from President

Assume the director received an email from the president, who requested that the director travel to another destination after the conference finishes to meet with the president of a training centre in Victoria, British Columbia.

- You will need to include the car rental information (name of company, address, and telephone number), ferry crossing information (time and address), hotel information (name, address, and telephone number), meeting information (name of company, name of contact, address, and telephone number), and revised flight information.

Car Rental

- Review the corporate policy for car rentals.
- Assume he picks up the rental car at a downtown location near the conference. Note: There may be a drop-off charge for returning the car to the Vancouver airport.
- Download the car rental information, which will include the address, hours of operation, type of vehicle selected, and cost.
- Print relevant information from the download.
- Attach the information to the itinerary.

Hotel

- Find a hotel that is close to the business meeting location in Victoria – you choose the hotel.
- Ensure you are checking him into a four-star hotel in a single room.
- Check TripAdvisor to see if there are any ratings on the hotel, and provide at least one TripAdvisor comment.
- Download the cost, address, phone number, and a picture of the hotel, if it is available.

- Print the relevant information from the download.
- Provide the hotel website address.
- Attach the information to the revised itinerary.

Driving Directions and Maps (Internet)

- Provide the following directions and maps:
  - From the car rental agency near the hotel to the ferry that crosses to Vancouver Island.
  - From the ferry to the hotel in Victoria.
  - From the hotel to the meeting with the president.
  - From the hotel back to the ferry to return to the mainland.
  - From the ferry landing to Vancouver airport.

Ferry

- Provide the ferry crossing times and fare schedules.
  Note: Do not forget there is both a vehicle and a passenger.

Flight

- Find the director a flight directly following the meeting (after 4 p.m.) to return home from Vancouver airport.

Revised Itinerary

- Revise your itinerary from Task 12 to include this change of plans from Task 18.

TASK 19   **TRAVEL CHECKLIST**

- Based on your knowledge from Tasks 1 through 18, prepare a travel checklist that you could use for future trips. Use check boxes such as ☐ to the left of the text.
- This checklist will enable you to plan future trips more effectively.

MAIL-OUTS AND SURVEYS

LEARNING OBJECTIVES

- Creating appointments
- Creating a task list
- Conducting research using the Internet
- Creating a database
- Drafting an invitation letter
- Merging letters
- Merging labels
- Editing a database
- Drafting a confirmation letter
- Creating a flyer
- Creating a survey in MS Word
- Creating a survey in SurveyMonkey

In this project, you will be planning a marketing fair, which will involve research, creating documents, and surveys.

Pop tasks will be assigned by your instructor as you make your way through this project. These are not identified in the learning objectives.

TASK 1	**APPOINTMENT**

RESOURCES: Calendar Software
Appendix D – Appointment Sample
Appendix E – Appointment Instructions
Appendix F – Interoffice Memorandum from Director of Marketing
and Sales

You have received an interoffice memorandum from the Director of Marketing and Sales regarding an upcoming marketing fair; he has asked you to organize this event for a date in February.

- Enter the event in the director's calendar.

TASK 2	**TASK LIST**

RESOURCE: Appendix F – Interoffice Memorandum from Director of Marketing
and Sales

To plan this event, it is essential that you create a task list to organize yourself.

- Using MS Word, create a list of tasks in a two-column table.
- The title of the first column will be "Task," and the title of the second column will be "Action Completed."
- In sequential order, list the items you will need to successfully plan and hold this event (based on the director's memo).
- The "Action Completed" column will be left blank at this point.

TASK 3	**RESEARCH**

RESOURCES: Appendix F – Memo from the Director of Marketing and Sales
Appendix F – Interoffice Memorandum from Director of Marketing
and Sales

To prepare the contact list, research must be undertaken using the Internet or telephone to determine the contact information. Present this information in an MS Word table.

- Determine the following information for ten companies in your city as outlined in the memo from the Director of Marketing and Sales:
  - Name of company
  - Address
  - Phone number
  - Fax number
  - Email address
  - Website
- Download this information from the Internet and copy/paste it into a Word document to prepare your recipient list through the MS Word Mailings feature.
- Create a fictitious name for each person.
- The person you are writing to is the Director of Human Resources.

TASK 4	**MAILINGS – RECIPIENT LIST – DATABASE**

To prepare for a mail-out, you must create a recipient list.

- Using the MS Word Mailings feature, prepare a recipient list detailing the information you gathered for the ten companies to create your contact list.
- Ensure that you customize your fields.

TASK 5	**MAILINGS – LETTER WITH MERGE FIELDS**

RESOURCES: Appendix C – Letterhead Template
Appendix D – Letter Sample

You must now create the letter to send to the recipients.

- Using the MS Word Mailings feature, compose a letter inviting five recipients (one from each sector) to the job marketing fair in February.
- The letter is from the Director of Marketing and Sales.
- The Director of Marketing and Sales is requesting that a representative from these companies come to speak at the fair. Please note that the Director of Human Resources for each company is the contact.
- Ensure that you use the company letterhead, and include in the body the purpose of event, date of event, times, location, length of presentation (20 minutes to speak and 10 minutes for questions), date to confirm participation, luncheon location, time of luncheon, and format of event.
- Indicate that a podium, a computer, and a projection unit are available, and ask recipients to indicate whether they will be using the computer for their presentations.
- Ensure that you save the merge field letter as a separate file.
- Merge showing all five recipient letters.

TASK 6	**MAILINGS – LABELS WITH MERGE FIELDS**

RESOURCE: Appendix E – Label Instructions

You will also require labels for the mail-out envelopes.

- Using the MS Word Mailings feature, produce a sheet of labels to the Directors of Human Resources for the five companies in this round of mail-outs.
- Use US Letter – Avery 5159 for your labels.
- Ensure that you save the merge field sheet of labels as a separate file.
- Merge showing all five recipients on one sheet.

TASK 7	**EDITING A RECIPIENT LIST – DATABASE**

RESOURCE: Appendix E – Editing a Merge Instructions

Assume that the five recipients on the first mail-out have confirmed their company participation at the job marketing fair.

- Delete the remaining five records from your recipient list.
- Add a field for the time slots that you will be allotting to each presenter.
- Note: They have 30 minutes each; do not forget the 15-minute coffee break.

TASK 8	**CONFIRMATION LETTER WITH MERGE FIELDS**

RESOURCES: Appendix C – Letterhead Template
Appendix D – Letter Sample

You are now in a position to send the confirmation to your five confirmed presenters.

- Prepare a new merge letter to the five confirmed presenting companies.
- The letter is from the Director of Marketing and Sales.
- Thank each Director of Human Resources for his or her commitment to send someone to attend.
- State the name and date of event.
- Include the time and location of luncheon again.
- Inform each company of the time slot allotted.
- Remind him or her that the presentation is 20 minutes plus 10 minutes for questions from the graduating students.
- Tell the Director of Human Resources you are looking forward to seeing him or her in February.
- Insert a "DRAFT" watermark.

TASK 9	**APPOINTMENTS**

RESOURCES: Calendar Software
Appendix D – Appointment Sample
Appendix E – Appointment Instructions

You must update the director's calendar with the new information.

- In the calendar, record the five 30-minute appointments, luncheon, and coffee break.
- Include the names of the presenters and their companies.

TASK 10	**FLYER**

RESOURCE: Appendix F – Interoffice Memorandum from Director of Marketing and Sales

For an event to be a success, you must ensure that it is advertised. You are hoping that most graduating students will attend.

- Create a one-page, letter-size flyer to post on the bulletin boards and to email to the graduating students.
- Include the following information:
  - Name of event
  - Date of event
  - Time of event
  - Location
  - Names of companies attending
  - Purpose of event
  - Note that refreshments will be served

- Use graphic lines, colour, the corporate logo, and anything else you think will make your flyer attractive.
- You want to convey a professional, desktop-published image, so be conscious of alignment and white space.

TASK 11

SURVEY

RESOURCES: Appendix D – Survey Samples
Appendix E – Survey Notes

The director has asked that you create a survey to give to the graduating students who attend. You have decided that you would like feedback on the following areas:

- Location of event
- Format of event
- Satisfaction with each presenter
- Length of time allotted
- Time of day
- Time of year

You have opted to create a paper survey using MS Word to hand to the graduates as they arrive for the marketing fair.

- Using the survey notes on key points for preparing a survey, create a survey consisting of no more than ten questions based on the areas listed above and any other question(s) you think would be beneficial.
- You must decide the proper way to ask the question to obtain the information you are seeking – i.e., open-ended questions; rankings; or yes/no/explain questions.
- Ensure that you date the survey.
- Ensure that you enumerate the questions.
- Ensure that you include a thank you for completing the survey.

TASK 12

SURVEYMONKEY

RESOURCES: Appendix D – Survey Samples
Appendix E – Survey Notes
Appendix E – SurveyMonkey Instructions

Another method of reaching the graduates is through SurveyMonkey, which is a free, easy-to-use, online software program.

- Using SurveyMonkey, create the survey from Task 11.

3

TABLES, CHARTS, AND REPORTS

LEARNING OBJECTIVES

- Creating a task
- Creating a budget template
- Creating tables using absolute cell references in projections
- Creating a fax cover
- Producing line, bar, and pie charts using MS Excel
- Formatting charts
- Creating a PowerPoint presentation
- Drafting an email
- Importing charts and tables into a report
- Keying a formal report (proposal) using MS Word with section breaks, a cover page, a table of contents, and appendices

In this project, you will be preparing a template for a budget for the company.

Berry, Duthie & Miller is relocating, and you will be creating data and charts to be represented in a PowerPoint presentation and report.

Pop tasks will be assigned by your instructor as you make your way through this project. These are not identified in the learning objectives.

TASK 1	**TASK**

RESOURCES: Calendar Software
Appendix D – Task Sample
Appendix F – Interoffice Memorandum from the Director of Finance

The Director of Finance has provided you with a draft budget form. He would like you to create a MS Excel spreadsheet so that he can prepare this year's budget. The deadline is in one week.

- Create a task to ensure that you meet your deadline.

TASK 2	**BUDGET**

RESOURCES: Appendix F – Interoffice Memorandum from Director of Finance
Appendix F – Draft Budget Form

You must prepare a professional-looking budget template.

- Using MS Excel and the draft budget form, create a template to be used by the director.
- Insert the company logo.
- Insert a title on the template: BDM Budget.
- Save the file as a template.
- Choose your own format.

TASK 3	**TABLES – PROJECTIONS AND REQUIREMENTS**

RESOURCES: Appendix D – Projection Table Using an Absolute Cell Reference Sample
Appendix F – Interoffice Memorandum from Director of Human Resources and Administration

You have been tasked with preparing the tables projecting the company's space requirements in five years. Also, you have been asked to input the projections into a table so that a real estate agent will be able to search for the best location.

The Director of Human Resources and Administration has provided you with information you require in the memo.

- Using MS Excel, prepare the three tables for staff growth, office space, and lease cost for rental beginning in January of next year.
  - Use separate worksheets for each table.
  - Use absolute cell references for the projections—the shortcut key is F4.
  - Use borders, fill, and different fonts to improve the look of your tables.
  - Use a comma separator where appropriate.
  - Use zero decimal places where appropriate as we will be working in whole numbers for results.
  - Centre each of the column headings.
  - Vertically and horizontally centre each spreadsheet.

- Rename the tables appropriately.
- Use all caps for the titles and centre.
- Under "Format Cells," choose "Text." This will format your cells as text and ensure that they appear exactly as you type them.

- Using the five-year projections that you have calculated, input the projected numbers into the requirements table for lease cost and square footage. This will ensure that the company does not outgrow the facility before the five-year lease has expired.
- Add in the other requirements needed for the new facility, and create a table that is user-friendly for the real estate agent.

TASK 4

FAX

RESOURCES: Appendix C – Fax Cover Template
Appendix D – Fax Cover Sample

Your current commercial real estate agent is Myles Blair of Royal Real Estate.

- Send Myles a fax from the Director of Human Resources and Administration. His fax number is 613-725-3423.
- Advise him that you are attaching the criteria chart as discussed last Friday.
- Give him a deadline of the end of next month to provide three locations that meet our needs.

If he needs further information or clarification, have him contact the Director of Human Resources and Administration.

TASK 5

CHARTS

RESOURCES: Tables from Task 3
Appendix C – Interoffice Memorandum Template
Appendix D – Interoffice Memorandum Sample

The Director of Human Resources and Administration popped by your desk and asked you to use the tables for staff growth, office space, and lease cost to prepare line, pie, and bar charts with the information for the projections each year. He is trying to decide which method to use to visually represent the data in the report.

- Create these nine charts as separate worksheets and then import them into MS Word so that you have all three types of charts per category on one page.
- You will have separate pages for staff growth, office space, and lease costs—three pages as one document.
- Insert a comment at the top of each of the three pages indicating which chart you would use to visually represent the data and why you chose that chart.
- Ensure that your charts are centred horizontally and that each is similar in size and in alignment.
- Prepare a memo to the Director of Human Resources and Administration attaching the charts.

TASK 6	**COMPARISON CHART**

RESOURCES: Requirements Table from Task 3
Appendix F – Letter from Real Estate Agent

Myles Blair has searched for a new office location and has provided three options. You have been tasked with updating the requirements chart from Task 3 to compare Options A, B, and C.

- Update the table with the new column headings as Requirements, Option A, Option B, and Option C.
- Include the actual information the real estate agent has provided.

TASK 7	**POWERPOINT**

RESOURCE: Pie Charts from Task 5

The Director of Human Resources and Administration has asked you to prepare a PowerPoint to email to the president, vice-presidents, and directors.

- Create a title slide with the title "Projections for New Office Location."
  - Include the company logo.
  - Include the current date.
- On the second slide, insert the company requirements you faxed to Myles Blair, the real estate agent.
- On the third, fourth, and fifth slides, insert the three pie charts for staff growth, office space, and lease cost created in Task 5.

TASK 8	**EMAIL**

RESOURCES: PowerPoint – Task 7
Appendix D – Email Sample

The PowerPoint presentation you created in Task 7 is the attachment to an email you must send to distribute the projections.

Prepare an email to the president, vice-presidents, and directors from the Director of Human Resources and Administration.

Include the following details in the body of the email:

- Refer to the attached PowerPoint presentation, indicating that it is a summary of the data that will be used to determine the new office location.
- Specify that the president has requested a meeting next Wednesday in the boardroom to make the final relocation decision, and has requested that everyone be in attendance.

TASK 9

REPORT

RESOURCES: Requirements Table from Task 3
Charts from Task 5
Appendix E – Reports
Appendix F – Draft Report

To have the final decision made and documented for the company and its employees, you have been tasked with preparing the proposal as a formal report.

- Using the draft report provided by the Director of Human Resources and Administration, prepare it in final format using MS Word, incorporating the charts and tables as requested.
- Fix any grammar or spelling errors.
- Include a title page with the name of the company, the title of the proposal, the date, and your name.
- Ensure that the report is one document incorporating the title page, table of contents, and report.
- Include a footer with the name of the proposal and the page number.
- Include a header with the name of the company and the logo.
- Use appropriate page numbering for the table of contents and the report itself.
- Insert side headings where appropriate.
- Generate the Table of Contents.

MEETINGS: INFORMAL, FORMAL, AND EXTERNAL

LEARNING OBJECTIVES

- Preparing a notice of meeting
- Scheduling a meeting
- Preparing an agenda
- Preparing a set of minutes
- Creating a contact
- Maintaining a document using tracking
- Taking minutes
- Annotating and highlighting correspondence
- Creating tasks
- Preparing a request for proposal
- Preparing a map and driving directions
- Preparing a memo
- Preparing a survey
- Online collaboration

In this project, you will be helping the Director of Training arrange the annual management committee meeting and retreat, which will take place at an offsite venue in March, 20xx.

Pop tasks will be assigned by your instructor as you make your way through this project. These are not identified in the learning objectives.

TASK 1	**NOTICE OF MEETING**

RESOURCES: Calendar Software
Appendix D – Notice of Meeting Sample
Appendix E – Meetings – An Introduction
Appendix E – Notices of Meetings Instructions
Appendix E – Scheduling Meetings Using MS Outlook

The first step in preparing for the retreat is to organize an **informal** meeting to plan the event. This is to be held on the last Friday in January, 20xx, at 1 p.m. in the Tamarack Boardroom. This meeting should last approximately 1.5 hours. The attendees include BDM's vice-presidents and directors.

- Prepare the notice of meeting. You would like agenda items submitted to you by the Monday of the same week on which the meeting is to take place. This notice is to be prepared as a meeting request in your calendar software.

TASK 2	**AGENDA (INFORMAL STYLE)**

RESOURCES: Appendix D – Agenda (Informal Style) Sample
Appendix E – Agenda Instructions

An agenda for the meeting needs to be prepared and distributed to all the attendees.

- Prepare an agenda using the informal style. The director has provided the following items for inclusion in the agenda:
  - Theme for the retreat
  - Retreat arrangements
  - Guest speaker
- Other items have already been submitted by directors and include:
  - Social activities (Director, Marketing and Sales)
  - Transportation to the venue (Director, Finance)
  - Menu options (Director, Finance)
  - Room assignments (Director, Human Resources and Administration)

TASK 3	**REVISING A SET OF MINUTES (INFORMAL STYLE)**

RESOURCES: Appendix D – Minutes (Informal Style) Sample
Appendix E – Minutes of Meetings Instructions
Appendix F – Draft Minutes (Informal Style)

The meeting has taken place. The Director of Training has forwarded his notes, which he would like you to use to prepare a set of minutes.

- Prepare a set of minutes based on the director's notes. Use the informal style.
- The director has advised you that the Vice-President of Operations was absent with regrets. All other directors were in attendance.
- Include action items where appropriate.
- Correct any errors in the director's notes regarding spelling, grammar, and format.

| TASK 4 | **CONTACT** |

RESOURCES: Calendar Software
Appendix D – Contact Sample
Appendix E – Formal Meetings Note

The Director of Finance has been asked to chair the upcoming BDM monthly board meeting. As a board meeting, the strict rules for a formal meeting need to be followed.

A notice will need to be prepared. But, before this is done, two new members have joined the board and need to be recorded as contacts. The members are:

- Douglas Carver, Partner, Mitchell Morecroft Chartered Accountants, 321 Moodie Drive, Ottawa, Ontario, K2H 9C4, phone 613-820-1008, fax 613-820-1882, email carverd@mmca.emp.ca.
- Elizabeth Drucker, Partner, Richardson-Labelle LLP, 1200 - 326 Albert Street, Ottawa, Ontario, K1R 0A5, phone 613-566-2012, fax 613-566-0022, email edrucker@richlaw.emp.ca.

| TASK 5 | **NOTICE (BY EVITE)** |

RESOURCES: Appendix E – Notices of Meetings Instructions
Appendix E – Notices of Meetings Using Evite Instructions
Appendix F – Draft Minutes (Formal Style)

The director has asked that you prepare a notice of meeting for a board meeting. This notice will be sent using an online program, Evite.

To determine the attendees, for the purposes of this workbook, you must review the draft minutes in Appendix F.

- Prepare a notice using Evite for the meeting. It is scheduled for the last Wednesday in January, at 7 p.m., and will run for approximately 2 hours. The location of the meeting is the Hudson Boardroom.
- Select an appropriate date by which agenda items must be submitted. The agenda items should be sent to you by email.

| TASK 6 | **AGENDA (FORMAL STYLE)** |

RESOURCES: Appendix D – Agenda (Formal Style) Sample
Appendix E – Agenda Instructions

An agenda for the board meeting needs to be prepared and distributed to all the attendees.

- Prepare an agenda in the formal style for the meeting.
- The following reports are to be included in the agenda:
  - Treasurer's Report
  - Recreation Committee Report
  - Grounds Committee Report
- The director has asked you to include the following topic as new business: new hires. The director also received the following topics from the members as new business: information management systems plan, from B. Bhatacharia; building renovations, from C. Crosby.

| TASK 7 | **MINUTES (FORMAL STYLE)** |

RESOURCES: Appendix D – Minutes (Formal Style) Sample
Appendix E – Minutes of Meetings Instructions
Appendix F – Draft Minutes (Formal Style)

You have taken the minutes to the board meeting. However, you need to prepare them in the formal style using complete sentences before distributing them.

- Prepare the minutes in the formal style.
- Use the details regarding time and location provided in Task 5.

| TASK 8 | **REVISION OF MINUTES (FORMAL STYLE) USING DOCUMENT TRACKING** |

RESOURCE: Appendix E – Document Tracking Instructions

Once the minutes are prepared, they are distributed so that each board member can review them to ensure accuracy. One tool that can be used to record and coordinate changes to the minutes made by all members is Track Changes, the document tracking feature in MS Word.

You will select a partner to record the changes made to a set of minutes. Each partner has been assigned the same tasks. However, one partner must complete the steps first as indicated in the section "Starting with the First Person," below. Once completed, the first partner will submit a copy of the assignment to the second partner. The second partner **cannot** proceed until this assignment is received.

Starting with the First Person

- Open the minutes prepared in Task 7.
- Turn on Track Changes.
- Move the last person in the Attendance list to the Absent list.
- Add George Strombo to the top of the Attendance list.
- Add two comments to the document using the New Comment button.
- Under New Business, delete the last item; this item was carried over in error from the last set of minutes.
- Under Next Meeting, change the date to the next day indicated.
- Save the document under the name "Formal Meeting Minutes Revised by [Your Name]" (use your own name). Submit a copy of the document to your partner.

The Second Person

- The second person now repeats the steps followed by the first person. Change George Strombo's name to George Black.

| TASK 9 | **TAKING MINUTES** |

RESOURCES: Appendix D – Minutes (Informal Style) Sample
Appendix E – Minutes of Meetings Instructions

An actual informal meeting will take place during class time. Your professor will take the role of chair for this meeting and you will be the secretary responsible for recording the minutes. You will convert your notes into a set of minutes.

- An agenda will be provided to you by your professor before the meeting, which should be used to help prepare the minutes.
- Prepare a set of minutes for the class meeting using the informal style.

TASK 10

HIGHLIGHTING AND ANNOTATING

RESOURCES: Appendix D – Highlighted and Annotated Letter Sample
Appendix E – External Meetings Instructions
Appendix E – Highlighting and Annotating Correspondence
Appendix F – Interoffice Memorandum from Director of Training

As you recall, the Director of Training has asked you to help arrange the upcoming annual management committee meeting and retreat in March. Because this will occur in the near future, you need to begin planning now.

The director has sent you a memo that provides you with the details of this event to help in planning. You will need to refer to this memo for this task and for Tasks 11 to 17.

- Using a highlighter, highlight the key points to plan the event. Note that these details will be used to help prepare the documents that are required in upcoming tasks.

TASK 11

TASKS

RESOURCES: Calendar Software
Appendix D – Task Sample
Appendix F – Interoffice Memorandum from Director of Training

You will be planning this event while you are performing your other duties in the office. The key to doing this successfully is to be very organized.

- Record the arrangements of the event as a single task. Ensure that you include a start date and a due date.

TASK 12

REQUEST FOR PROPOSAL

RESOURCES: Appendix C – Request for Proposal Template
Appendix D – Request for Proposal Sample
Appendix E – Request for Proposal (RFP) Note
Appendix E – Request for Proposal Template with Explanation
Appendix F – Interoffice Memorandum from Director of Training

You are required to find the most suitable venue for the event. This will be based on a combination of factors, including location, available amenities, and cost.

To establish this, you are to prepare a Request for Proposal that will be submitted to potential venues. Note: For the purposes of this task, you will be asked to complete the form for one venue only, as directed by your professor. Although most of the details are completed by a contact person at the venue, you must include certain details to ensure a proper response. The details that you are to provide include:

- Method of submission (e.g., mail or fax)
- Deadline for response

- Contact details for submission
- General meeting requirements (i.e., date(s) during which the event will be held and the number of participants)
- Meeting space (dates and times required, style and type of room, and the number of participants)
- Equipment and furniture requirements
- Service requirements (setup and cleanup)
- Accommodation dates required
- Number of rooms required
- Room type requested
- Parking requirements
- Amenities preferred (pool and fitness room)
- Menu requirements

TASK 13 — NOTICE OF MEETING

RESOURCES: Calendar Software
Appendix D – Notice of Meeting (External) Sample
Appendix E – Notices of Meetings Instructions
Appendix E – Scheduling Meetings Using MS Outlook
Appendix F – Interoffice Memorandum from Director of Training

The director has asked that you prepare a notice of meeting for the event.

- Prepare a notice of meeting as a meeting request using your calendar software.
- The notice should be sent to all the directors, the executive assistant, and you.
- This notice should inform the attendees of the name of the meeting, dates, location, transportation arrangements, room reservations, check-in time, and dinner reservation for the first night.

TASK 14 — AGENDA (CONFERENCE OR SEMINAR STYLE)

RESOURCES: Appendix D – Agenda (Conference or Seminar Style) Sample
Appendix E – Agenda Instructions
Appendix F – Draft Agenda
Appendix F – Interoffice Memorandum from Director of Training

The director has attached a draft agenda for the event to the memo; however, it contains a number of inconsistencies.

- Revise the agenda using the conference or seminar style.

TASK 15 — MAP AND DRIVING DIRECTIONS

RESOURCES: Internet Map Site
Appendix F – Interoffice Memorandum from Director of Training

The participants will be arranged into carpools and drive to the venue. As a result, they should be provided with information on how to get from Albert Street to the venue.

- Print a map that clearly shows the route the drivers should take. Street names should be visible.
- Include detailed instructions on how to get to the venue.

TASK 16 — INTEROFFICE MEMORANDUM

RESOURCES: Appendix C – Interoffice Memorandum Template
Appendix D – Interoffice Memorandum Sample
Appendix F – Interoffice Memorandum from Director of Training

The director has requested an update on the arrangements you have made for the event.

- Prepare a memo advising the director of the arrangements you have made. Note that the details should be described in paragraph format and not as a list.
- Include the following details:
  - Number of rooms booked
  - Room cost per night
  - Check-in time
  - Check-out time
  - Hotel and meeting services
  - Date and time for which for meeting room is reserved
  - Reservation of a computer projection unit and screen
  - Order for meals and refreshments for breaks (morning and afternoon)
  - Reservation for 7:30 p.m. at the _____ restaurant for the first night
  - Reservation for 7:30 p.m. at the _____ restaurant for the second night

---

TASK 17 — SURVEYMONKEY

RESOURCES: Appendix D – Survey – Paper Format
Appendix E – Survey – Paper Format Notes
Appendix E – SurveyMonkey Instructions
Appendix F – Interoffice Memorandum from Director of Training

This year's external event was a resounding success. However, you decide that next year's event should be even better. You will prepare a survey to solicit the participants' feedback on the event one week after the event.

- Using SurveyMonkey, prepare a survey that includes eight to ten questions using two different question types (e.g., multiple choice or comment/essay). Questions may relate to desired venue, location, type of transportation, guest speakers, and theme of conference.

TASK 18   **ONLINE COLLABORATION USING JOIN.ME**

RESOURCES: Appendix E – Join.me for Online Collaboration Instructions
                          Appendix G – Teleconferencing PowerPoint Presentation

The president is currently out of the office on business; however, a briefing on the event has been requested. The president has decided that an online collaboration would be the most efficient method for this briefing.

- Using **Join.me**, conduct an online collaboration with a partner. Before you begin, one of you needs to assume the role of chair and the other the role of the participant.

- The chair should initiate the meeting by downloading the application and by copying and pasting the viewer link in an email that is sent to the participant.

- Once the email is received, the participant joins the meeting by copying the **Join.me** link in the body of the email to the address bar in Internet Explorer.

- Both the chair and the participant should use the **Chat** feature to discuss the event.

- The chair should open the Online Collaboration PowerPoint Presentation and key the names of both the chair and the participant on the first slide.

- The chair should give the presentation by advancing through each slide.

- The participant should use the **Chat** feature to request control of the screen; the chair should provide this control.

- The participant should perform at least two modifications to the presentation (e.g., additions or deletions).

- The chair should stop sharing the screen and send a copy of the modified presentation to the participant. The participant should accept the presentation and save it.

- The partners should now reverse the roles (i.e., Partner 1 should be the participant and Partner 2 should become the chair) and repeat the steps above.

JOB SEARCH

LEARNING OBJECTIVES

- Creating business cards
- Creating a personal list inventory
- Researching potential employers
- Job search tracking
- Designing a résumé
- Applying for a job online
- Preparing two types of cover letters: prospecting and solicited
- Researching interview questions
- Conducting mock interviews
- Preparing a portfolio
- Creating a thank-you letter
- Post-interview reflection

In this project, you have been asked by the Director of Training to create and conduct a job search workshop. To prepare for the job search workshop, you will need to research and experience all the steps in finding a position.

Job search pop tasks will supplement your research for the workshop. These pop tasks will be assigned by your instructor and are not identified in the learning objectives.

TASK 1	**BUSINESS CARD**

RESOURCES: Appendix D – Business Cards Sample
Appendix E – Business Cards

A job search effort should include more than just scanning newspapers for job advertisements. Networking is a great way to find out about job opportunities. An excellent tool for networking is a personal job search business card that includes your own information (address, phone number, and email address).

Both the résumé and business card are exceptional self-marketing tools. However, unlike a résumé, business cards can be brought to any social situation because of their size and portability.

- Create your own business card to be included as an example in the job search package.

TASK 2	**PERSONAL LIST OF SKILLS INVENTORY**

RESOURCES: Appendix D – Action Verbs (for Résumés and Cover Letters)
Appendix E – Personal Skills Inventory

Before a résumé can be created, you should create a list of your personal skills. To make this list, you should consider strong vocabulary that catches the reader's eye and encourages further reading.

- Research action verbs used in résumés and cover letters.
- Using the Internet, determine five sites where other lists of vocabulary for résumés are included.
- Create a personal skills list composed of a minimum of five action verbs that best describe each of your skills. These words will be used in your résumé.

TASK 3	**RESEARCHING INDUSTRY**

RESOURCE: Appendix E – Researching Potential Employers

Using the Internet, you can conduct research to determine where you might want to work and the type of position that interests you.

- Use the Internet to find five companies or organizations where you might be interested in working.
- List the company names, addresses, phone numbers, fax numbers, email addresses, website addresses, and any other contact information you can find on their websites.
- Write a paragraph or two in full sentence format on what you discovered about these companies and indicate why you selected them.

TASK 4	**JOB SEARCH TRACKING**

RESOURCE: Appendix D – Job Search Tracking Sample

Organizational skills are very important in any job search. You need to keep track of the companies to which you have sent applications and your status in the job search process with each one. A comprehensive job search tracking table can be used to record this information.

- Draft a job search tracking table that includes sections to document the following information:
  - The organizations to which you have applied (the name and contact information)
  - The dates on which you have made your applications
  - A brief description of the response received from each organization
- Add the details of each of the five companies from Task 3.

TASK 5

DESIGNING A RÉSUMÉ

RESOURCES: Appendix D –Résumé – Chronological – Sample
Appendix D –Résumé – Functional – Sample
Appendix E – Résumé Writing

You feel comfortable with your personal skills inventory and you know where you want to apply.

Create a résumé to showcase the skills you wish to emphasize for the organizations to which you are applying. Based on your knowledge of chronological and functional résumés, select the format that you believe is the most appropriate for you.

TASK 6

APPLYING ONLINE

RESOURCES: Appendix D – Job Application Form
Appendix E – Applying Online

The Internet represents an excellent source for potential jobs. There are a number of job boards that advertise jobs on behalf of companies and organizations. Many larger organizations host websites that list available jobs. Most of these websites provide you with the ability to apply for these jobs online.

- You are to find and review three job sites that accept online applications. Write a summary paragraph on how to apply online. In your summary, ensure that you do the following:
  - Name the three job sites for online applications.
  - Describe each of the three job sites and specify whether they are user-friendly.
  - Explain the process for applying to each of the three positions.
  - Provide three characteristics that distinguish online applications from mailed applications.
  - Provide one reason why online applying is more efficient and one reason why online applying is less efficient than sending in a résumé.

TASK 7

COVER LETTER

RESOURCES: Appendix D – Cover Letter (Prospecting) – Sample
Appendix D – Cover Letter (Solicited) – Sample
Appendix E – Cover Letters

The function of the cover letter is to encourage someone to read your résumé. The cover letter also serves as a way to introduce you and your résumé. Ensure that the letterhead on your cover letter and résumé is the same.

- Choose one of the companies you researched in Task 3 and create two different cover letters (A and B) that you will use to apply to this organization.
  - Cover letter A is a prospecting cover letter inquiring about any position that may be available.
  - Cover letter B is a solicited cover letter that is used when applying for a position that you have determined is available through a job website, local newspaper, or an acquaintance you know who works in the organization. Please choose a company of your choice that differs from Cover letter A.

TASK 8

RESEARCHING INTERVIEW QUESTIONS

RESOURCE: Appendix D – Interview Question Examples

Your application has made the grade! Now you need to prepare for the interview. This requires much advance preparation.

- Use the Internet to find five websites that discuss types of interviews and interview questions.
- Prepare a list that includes the name, the address, and a brief description of each of these websites.
- Select three interview questions from these websites.
- Write a paragraph on why you think these questions would be appropriate in your preparation for interviews with organizations.

TASK 9

MOCK INTERVIEWS

RESOURCE: Method of Interview (Suggestions Include: Phone, iPad, Computer, Video Camera, or Live)

A mock interview is an excellent way to prepare for an interview. You will have the opportunity to practise answering typical interview questions and master your presentation skills.

- Select a partner to conduct a mock interview. In this interview, you will be the job applicant and your partner will be the interviewer.
- Use the three questions you selected in Task 8 to practise for an interview.
- Now conduct the mock interview. This interview is to be conducted in person, and videotaped with a cell phone, computer video software, or a video camera (your instructor will indicate which method you will use).
- Your partner is to ask you one interview question from your list of three questions.
- Now reverse roles (i.e., your partner will be the job applicant and you will be the interviewer).

TASK 10

PORTFOLIO

RESOURCE: Appendix E – Portfolio

A portfolio is a useful tool to take with you on an interview. The portfolio should include documents and other artifacts that serve as a testament to the skills and experience you have described in your résumé.

The portfolio could be used by you during the interview to provide evidence of a required skill or by the interviewer after the interview to validate your skills and experience. For it to be effective, the work that you include should be completely free of errors and logically arranged.

- Consider 15 business documents you have prepared that represent an overall summary of this office simulation.
- If necessary, update the documents by correcting any errors and by including any new information you may have acquired since you created the documents.
- Ensure the portfolio is professionally formatted. Consider a theme for your portfolio. What type of paper will you use throughout? What font type and size will you use? Will you have a logo on every page? Use headers and footers to highlight your name and for page numbering.
- Assemble the 15 documents according to the directions of your professor.
- Organize the documents in a way that will allow you or the interviewer to quickly access examples, either during the interview or afterward.
- Create a table of contents.
- Create a title page that includes your name and contact information.

TASK 11

THANK-YOU LETTER

RESOURCE: Appendix D – Thank-You Letter Sample

When an interview is completed, you need to send a thank-you letter immediately.

- Create a thank-you letter for one of the five organizations you have researched. Assume that you have had an interview with this organization.
- Use the same letterhead that you used on your cover letter and résumé. Consistency is important.
- Research common interview questions. Choose three. Assume that these three were questions asked during your interview. Reflect on how you would have answered these three questions showcasing your strengths. These strengths should be included in the body of your thank-you letter.

TASK 12

POST-INTERVIEW

RESOURCE: Appendix D – Post-Interview Job Search Tracking Sample

After an interview, you need to take time to reflect on your performance. This will assist you during future interviews.

- Add a row to your job search tracking table. Label this section "Post-Interview Notes." Take the time to fill in this section with information you now have after your interview.
- Complete this section based on an experience you had at an actual interview or the mock interview. Consider some or all of the following questions to help you record your thoughts.
  - Did you arrive early for the interview?
  - Did you have to wait outside the interviewing room? If so, was the organization's atmosphere positive?
  - Who interviewed you? Include names and titles.

- How long was the interview?
- What are three questions you can remember from the interview?
- How comfortable were you during the interview?
- What areas did you feel you were not prepared to discuss in this interview?
- What do you need to do more research on before you have another interview?
- Do you feel your résumé is complete and has all the necessary details for any interview?
- Now that the interview is over, do you think you would like to pursue a position at this organization, if you receive an offer?
- Do you have any other comments you want to note about this interview?

Project 6

INTERNATIONAL TRAVEL ARRANGEMENTS

LEARNING OBJECTIVES

- Making international travel arrangements
- Conducting research using the Internet
- Performing currency conversions
- Calculating time differences
- Researching international travel costs
- Preparing a travel authorization
- Scheduling an appointment
- Creating a contact
- Creating a task
- Drafting a confirmation letter
- Renewing a Canadian passport
- Preparing a travel itinerary
- Drafting an email
- Drafting a letter
- Preparing an international travel checklist
- Drafting an interoffice memorandum

In this project, you will be making the necessary arrangements for the Director of Marketing and Sales to attend an international tradeshow.

Pop tasks will be assigned by your instructor as you make your way through this project. These are not identified in the learning objectives.

| TASK 1 | **ONLINE RESEARCH** |

RESOURCES: Appendix E – Travel (International) Arrangements
Appendix F – Letter of Invitation
Appendix G – International Travel Arrangements Research Table

The Director of Marketing and Sales has received an invitation to attend the Retail Expo in Hong Kong. He has asked you to begin making the necessary arrangements. The first step is to conduct research to provide the director with background information on his destination.

- Using the table provided, answer questions that will provide the director with some background information on his destination. Include the URL for each of the websites where the information was found.

| TASK 2 | **CURRENCY EXCHANGE** |

RESOURCE: Appendix E – Travel (International) Arrangements

The director will require some cash to cover a number of initial expenses upon his arrival in Hong Kong. The currency that is used in Hong Kong is different from that used in Canada. As a result, you will need to convert the cash required from Canadian to Hong Kong funds.

- You have determined that the director needs $200 Canadian. Based on the rate to exchange Canadian dollars into the currency used in Hong Kong, as determined in question 15 on the research table, what is $200 Canadian in the currency used in Hong Kong?

- Next, assume that the director has arrived back in Ottawa from Hong Kong. He has $50 Canadian in Hong Kong currency that he would like to exchange into Canadian dollars.
  - What is the rate to exchange Hong Kong currency into Canadian dollars?
  - What is $50 Canadian in Hong Kong currency?

| TASK 3 | **TIME ZONE** |

RESOURCE: Appendix E – Travel (International) Arrangements

The director will be travelling to a different time zone when he goes to Hong Kong. Each time zone is a geographic area with a different standard or "local" time. If you need to call the director while he is away, you will need to consider the time difference between your zone and his to ensure that he is available to take the call.

- Assume that you need to call the director while he is at the tradeshow in Hong Kong. There is a discrepancy in a sales contract that needs to be dealt with immediately. You assume he'll be in his room by 9 p.m. and decide to time your call for that time. What would the time be in Ottawa when you place this call?

- At noon on the day before travelling back to Ottawa, the director decides he would like to stay an extra day in Hong Kong to sightsee. But, changing his travel plans requires that he call the president for authorization. What time would it be in Ottawa when he places this call? Assuming that the president doesn't have any appointments outside the office, would she likely be at the office to receive the call?

| TASK 4 | **TRAVEL BUDGET** |

RESOURCES: Appendix B – Corporate Policies
Appendix D – Travel Expenses Table Sample
Appendix F – Letter of Invitation

You need to prepare a travel authorization for the trip. The travel authorization provides details regarding the trip including the purpose, destination, travel arrangements, and budget. Preparation of this document is necessary when seeking approval for travel from the responsible manager.

The first step in preparing the travel authorization will be to conduct research to determine the cost of the trip. Expenses will include the flight, hotel, meals, miscellaneous expenses, tradeshow fee, and ground transportation both at home and at the tradeshow location.

First, conduct research to determine the following expenses.

Flights

- The director would like to minimize the number of stopovers and would like to book his seat in advance.
- He will be leaving on the Friday prior to the tradeshow.
- As per corporate policy, he will fly economy class.
- He will be returning the day after the tradeshow.
- Download this information detailing the cost and flight schedule.

Hotel

- Using the information from the hotel's website, determine the total cost for the director's stay. Select the best available rate.

Ground Transportation

- The director will be using taxi chits to and from the airport in Ottawa.
- As per corporate policy, he will require a single room.
- Determine whether there is a hotel shuttle in Hong Kong for the trip to and from the airport. If so, determine the cost. If not, determine how much a taxi would cost to and from the airport.

Now, you'll want to summarize these expenses.

Cost Chart

- Based on the details below, and the research you conducted above, prepare a table of your costs indicating the name and amount of each expense:
  - The meal per diem is $50.
  - The miscellaneous amount (e.g., tips) is $100.
  - The tradeshow registration fee is in the invitation letter.
  - The airfare is based on your research above.
  - The total hotel cost is based on your research above.
  - The ground transportation in Ottawa is $45 each way.
  - The ground transportation in Hong Kong is determined by your research above.

TASK 5	**TRAVEL AUTHORIZATION**

RESOURCES: Appendix C – Travel Authorization Template
Appendix E – Travel Authorization Template with Explanation

Check with the director to ensure that he is satisfied with your proposed arrangements. Then, prepare the travel authorization. As you are completing this document, refer to the details below:

- You will need to do currency conversions as funds are in Canadian dollars.
- He would like $200 Canadian as a travel advance to cover miscellaneous expenses such as tips, ground transportation, and some meals.
- The purpose of the trip is to participate in a trade expo and to investigate potential business opportunities.
- His employee number is 556720.
- His cost centre is 7522.
- The account number is 3117-00, which is the convention/conference account.

TASK 6	**APPOINTMENT**

RESOURCES: Calendar Software
Appendix D – Appointment Sample
Appendix E – Appointment Instructions
Appendix F – Letter of Invitation

Assume that the director plans to leave the Saturday before the tradeshow and to return the day after. You should block this time in the director's calendar.

- Enter the appointment in the director's calendar.
- The following details should be included: the name of the tradeshow, tradeshow location, hotel name, addresses, telephone and fax numbers, and website addresses. Ensure that the telephone numbers are recorded as direct dial numbers from Canada. You will need to go to the websites for both the tradeshow and the hotel to determine some of these details.

TASK 7	**CONTACT**

RESOURCES: Calendar Software
Appendix D – Contact Sample

As always, the director updates his contacts based on his current working relationships.

- Create a new contact for the person sending the invitation to the director.

TASK 8	**TASK**

RESOURCES: Calendar Software
Appendix D – Task Sample

You will be making arrangements for this trip while performing your other responsibilities. Organization will be the key to your success. One task you will need to remember to complete soon is a response to the letter of invitation.

- Create a task to reply to the letter by the appropriate date. It should have a start and due date. Remember that it takes some time to mail correspondence to Hong Kong. Ensure that you leave a minimum of two weeks in advance for mailing.

TASK 9	**REPLY TO INVITATION**

RESOURCES: Appendix C – Letterhead Template
Appendix D – Letter Sample

You are now in a position to confirm the director's attendance at the tradeshow.

- Draft a letter on behalf of the director confirming his attendance.
- Include the name of the tradeshow, location, dates, conference identification number, and the payment information for the tradeshow.

TASK 10	**CANADIAN PASSPORT**

RESOURCES: Appendix E – Travel (International) Arrangements
Appendix G – Passport Table

A Canadian passport is an essential document for international travel. The director's passport has expired; you will need to advise him on the steps required to renew the passport.

- Please answer the questions in the Passport table to learn more about this important document.
- Based on the following details, determine whether or not the director is eligible to renew his passport:
  - He is a Canadian citizen.
  - He lives in Ottawa, Ontario.
  - He was 32 years old at the time of his previous passport application.
  - He has never reported his passport lost or stolen.
  - His current passport is in pristine condition.
  - He was living in Vancouver, BC when he submitted his previous application.
  - His previous passport was valid for five years.
  - His passport was issued six years ago today.
  - He is submitting this current application under the same name.

TASK 11	**TRAVEL ITINERARY**

RESOURCE: Appendix D – Travel Itinerary – International – Sample
Appendix F – Letter of Invitation

Prepare an itinerary for the trip. The itinerary is a detailed plan for the trip that ensures that the traveller knows the dates, times, and locations for all activities and events. You will need to refer to the letter of invitation for details. Be sure you include the following information:

- Flight times and flight numbers from your research
- Ground transportation
- Hotel contact information
- Tradeshow information

In addition, the director plans to go sight-seeing on the Monday after he arrives. On Tuesday, he will be meeting with a representative of the Hong Kong Institute of Marketing, Mr. Angel Leung, to inquire about becoming a corporate member. He is scheduled to meet with Mr. Leung from 8:30 a.m. to 11:30 a.m. The address for the Institute is 3/F, 88 Commercial Building, 28 - 34 Wing Lok Street, Hong Kong, and the phone number is (852) 2881-6682.

TASK 12

EMAIL

RESOURCE: Appendix D – Email Sample

Assume that it is the last Monday in April. The director's colleagues should be informed of his impending absence.

- Prepare an email to the president, the vice-presidents, and the other directors advising them of the director's upcoming absence. Include the purpose and specific dates for his trip. Also indicate that the Director of Finance, Nathan Black, will be acting in his absence.

TASK 13

LETTER

RESOURCES: Appendix C – Letterhead Template
Appendix D – Letter Sample

The director would like to increase Berry, Duthie & Miller's Asian presence. To that end, the director hopes to meet with a potential partner.

- Prepare a letter from the director to Anliza Mak, Business Consultant, Management Development Services (MDS) Ltd. Include the following details:
  - Inform Ms. Mak that the director will be travelling to Hong Kong for the retail expo.
  - Inquire as to whether a meeting would be possible.
  - Berry, Duthie & Miller is looking to expand its market into Hong Kong and is hoping to develop a partnership with MDS Ltd.
  - Provide the dates the director will be in Hong Kong.
  - Indicate where he will be staying.
  - Include any other information you think may be significant or ask any questions that you think are necessary.

TASK 14

MEMO

RESOURCES: Appendix C – Interoffice Memorandum Template
Appendix D – Interoffice Memorandum Sample
Appendix E – Travel (International) Arrangements

The Vice-President of Operations is responsible for both domestic and international travel. He would like you to prepare a travel checklist that will be used for future international trips.

- Prepare a memo to the Vice-President of Operations in which you identify the tasks you feel need to be completed to ensure a successful trip overseas. These tasks may be presented in bullet format.

Appendix A

Organization Chart

ORGANIZATION CHART

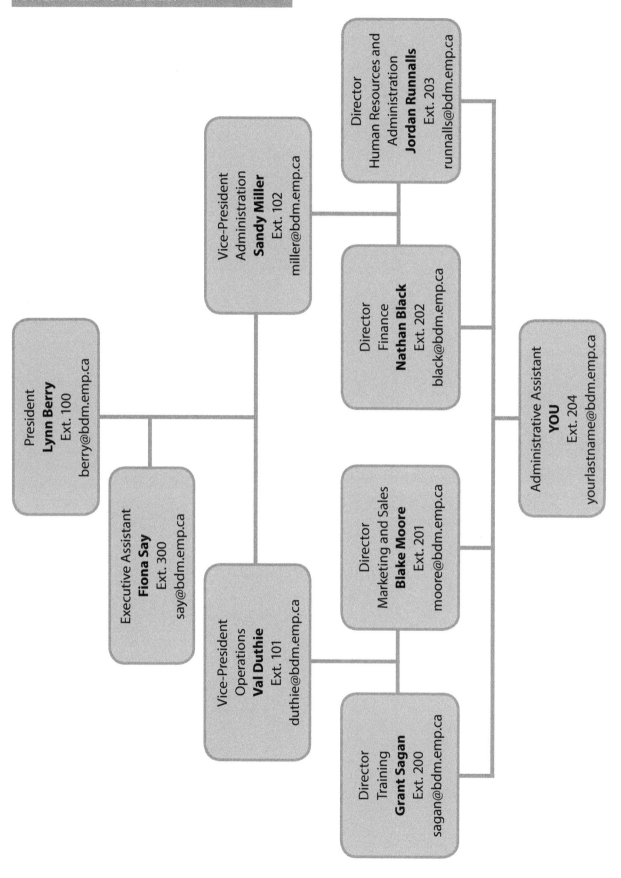

Appendix B

Corporate Policies

CORPORATE POLICIES

Airline Flights
Air Canada is the preferred carrier for international travel; however, when finding domestic flights, always check and provide information on a comparable WestJet flight (airport locations, times, flight numbers, and costs). Air Canada Tango is used on domestic flights. Direct flights are preferred, and seats should be booked in advance. Company policy is to fly economy class. Berry, Duthie & Miller has an account with Air Canada for business flights.

Car Rentals
Berry, Duthie & Miller uses Avis Car Rental. All rentals must be in the economy category. Ask Avis for their Full Service option (car is returned to an Avis location without filling gas tank). Auto insurance is covered by the corporate credit card, which is used for full payment of any car rental.

Corporate Credit Card
The American Express card is the corporate credit card. This card is a privilege not a right, and is distributed to those employees who incur many expenses as a result of their position. Any personal expenses incurred should be paid using the employee's personal credit card.

Corporate Entertaining
Corporate credit card charges for business entertaining must not exceed $400 without approval of the president.

Hotels
Berry, Duthie & Miller uses the Westin chain of hotels where possible. All hotel charges will be paid with the corporate credit card unless the charges are for a tradeshow that is paid in advance by corporate cheque. Company policy is to book a single room.

Meal Allowance
A $50 per diem allowance is provided for business travel. Alcoholic beverages are not to be included in any corporate expenses. Receipts are required to substantiate expenses.

Personal Vehicle
When a personal vehicle is used for business travel, the driver will be reimbursed 45 cents per kilometre.

Phone Calls
Employees will be distributed a corporate cellular phone when the position entails phone calls outside of the office. Any employee travelling outside of the office must pay his or her own expenses for personal phone calls from hotels.

Private Accommodation
When an employee obtains private accommodation when travelling, a $50 per diem is allotted.

Taxi
Taxi chits are available with Blue Line taxi for local transportation.

Appendix C

Templates

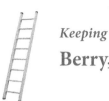

Keeping You in the Game
Berry, Duthie & Miller

820 - 360 Albert Street
Ottawa, ON K1R 7X7

info@bdm.emp.ca

613-237-9482 (telephone)
613-237-9400 (fax)

www.bdm.emp.ca

FAX

To:

Fax No.:

Date:

From:

No. of pages (including cover page):

If pages are missing, please contact:

Comments:

Keeping You in the Game

Berry, Duthie & Miller

INTEROFFICE MEMORANDUM

To:

From:

Date:

Subject:

LETTERHEAD

Keeping You in the Game

Berry, Duthie & Miller

820 - 360 Albert Street
Ottawa, ON K1R 7X7

info@bdm.emp.ca

613-237-9482 (telephone)
613-237-9400 (fax)

www.bdm.emp.ca

Berry, Duthie & Miller

REQUEST FOR PROPOSAL

Submission Requirements

Submission Due Date	Time
Submission Method	

Contact Information

General	
Company/Organization Name	
Address 1	
Address 2	
City	Province
Postal Code	
Contact Person	
Salutation	
Last Name	First Name
Phone	Fax
Email Address	
Fax Number	Email
Web Address	

Facility Information

General	
Name	
Address	
City	Province
Postal Code	Phone

REQUEST FOR PROPOSAL (Page 2)

General Meeting Requirements

Meeting Name	
Dates	
Function Start Date	Function End Date
Arrival Date	Departure Date
Number of People	
Notes	

Meeting Room(s)

General		
Start Date	End Date	
Capacity	Setup Type	
Equipment and Furniture		
☐ Chairs	☐ Tables	☐ Microphone
☐ Projector	☐ Videotaping	☐ Wireless Internet Access
☐ Screen	☐ Video Projector	
Other (Specify)		
Services		
☐ Setup	☐ Cleanup	☐ Other

Accommodations

Check-in Time	Check-out Time
Single Number Required	Cost per night
Double Number Required	Cost per night
Suite Number Required	Cost per night
Notes	

Amenities

☐ Business Services	☐ Fitness Centre	☐ Golf
☐ High Speed Internet	☐ Indoor Pool	☐ Outdoor Pool
☐ Parking		
Other		

Food and Beverage

Type	Required	Cost of each	Description/Notes (i.e., if event is +1 day, indicate dates required)
Breakfast	☐	$	
Lunch	☐	$	
Reception	☐	$	
Dinner	☐	$	
Breaks	☐	$	

Berry, Duthie & Miller
Travel Authorization

General Information

Name:	Employee No.:
Position:	Department:

Party to Visit:
Location:
Purpose of Trip:

From:	To:

Estimated Cost

Account No.	Cost Centre	Location	Amount

Transportation

Air: ☐ Yes ☐ No	Rail: ☐ Yes ☐ No	Car: ☐ Yes ☐ No	Other:
Describe:			

Accommodation

Required: ☐ Yes ☐ No	Number of Nights:	From:	To:
Preferred:	(1)	(2)	(3)

Travel Advance

Date Required:	Canadian	U.S.	Other
Cash (Max $150)			
Company Cheque			
Travellers' Cheques			
Total Advance			
Foreign Exchange			
Canadian Equivalent			

Authorization

Employee Signature:	Date:	Authorized By:	Date:

BERRY, DUTHIE & MILLER TRAVEL EXPENSE CLAIM

CLAIMANT _____   Employee No. _____   Party visited

Purpose of trip _____   Date of claim _____   Lcn/city _____

Province _____

For period from: _____   Country _____

_____ to _____ inclusive

EXPENSES PAID BY CLAIMANT				HST	TOTALS

1   Claimant's auto   km @ _____ $0.45 /km)

(itemize on sheet 2)

2   Other transportation

Date	Carrier	Ticket No.	Amount

3   Accommodation

Date	City	Hotel/Motel	Amount

4   Meals and related gratuities (itemize on sheet 2)

5   Other expenses (itemize on sheet 2)

6   Total expenses paid by claimant

7   Deduct cash advance(s)

8   Balance owed to:

     Claimant [ ]   Company [ ]

EXPENSES CHARGED TO BDM			Amount	
Date	Description	Ticket No.	Canada	Outside
9	Total Expenses Charged to BDM			

TOTAL EXPENSES (line 6 plus 9)

Acc't No.	Cost Centre	Location	Amount	Accounting Use Only
				T.V. Number
				Claim Number
				TAX (Meals)

Claimant: I hereby certify that this claim is correct in all respects and in accordance with company policy, and that expenses claimed were actually incurred on BDM business.

were actually incurred on BDM & Associates business.

Signature

Date

TOTAL _____

Recommended _____ Date _____

Approved _____ Date _____

Send original to Travel (attach receipts, ticket stubs, etc. as required by Policy 5.14)

TRAVEL EXPENSE CLAIM (Page 2)

SPENT IN CANADA							SPENT OUTSIDE CANADA					
MEAL EXPENSES							MEAL EXPENSES					
Date	Location	B'kfast	Lunch	Dinner	TOTAL		Date	Location	B'kfast	Lunch	Dinner	TOTAL

HST			TOTAL to line 4 sheet 1							TOTAL to line 4 sheet 1	
Date	Description of other expenses (in Canada)			Km (line 1)	Other (line 5)	Date	Description of other expenses (outside Canada)				Other (line 5)
HST				TOTAL						TOTAL	

sheet 2 — Record all expenses in Canadian funds. Do not extract HST from receipts.

VOICE MESSAGE

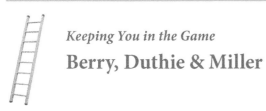

Keeping You in the Game

Berry, Duthie & Miller

VOICE MESSAGE

To:

From:

Time:

Date:

Subject:

Message:

Appendix D

Sample Documents

ACTION VERBS (FOR RÉSUMÉS AND COVER LETTERS)

- activated
- altered
- applied
- assembled
- arranged
- catalogued
- classified
- collected
- communicated
- compiled
- composed
- created
- described
- designed
- developed
- drafted
- edited
- estimated
- gathered
- generated
- implemented
- inspected
- listed
- maintained
- monitored
- operated
- organized
- planned
- prepared
- presented
- processed
- proofread
- purchased
- recorded
- retrieved
- summarized
- updated

HR MANAGEMENT CONFERENCE

Agenda
Rockeries Hotel and Conference Centre
November 12 to 13, 20xx

Tuesday, November 12

0900 – 1000	Registration and Breakfast Sponsored by Ironside Inc.	Bateman Hall
1000 – 1100	Opening Remarks from the Chair/ Speaker: Joanne Harrison, CEO, The HR Management Team	Auditorium
1100 – 1200	Motivating Employees Speaker: Leonard Rhymer	Tennison Hall
1200 – 1300	Lunch; Networking	Dining Room
1300 – 1345	Online Recruitment Issues Speaker: Loretta Swenson	Tennison Hall

Wednesday, November 13

0800 – 0900	Breakfast and Address by Vice-President, Suzanne Ross	Bateman Hall
0900 – 1100	Closing Remarks by President, Frank Biltman	Auditorium

INFORMATION TECHNOLOGY ADVISORY COMMITTEE

Agenda
Monthly Meeting
Thursday, November 18, 20xx
11 a.m.
Conference Room, 3rd Floor

1. Call to Order

2. Approval of Agenda

3. Approval of Previous Meeting Minutes

4. Old Business

5. Reports

    a. Employee Satisfaction Survey Results — R. McDonald

    b. Report on Computer Upgrades for 20xx — S. McKennirey

    c. Report on Budget Training — M. Fields

6. New Business

    a. Discussion of 20xx Budget

7. Date of Next Meeting

8. Adjournment

AGENDA (INFORMAL STYLE)

Agenda
Monthly Sales Meeting
Conference Board Room
September 21, 20xx
9 a.m.

1. Sales results for the third quarter — D. Rhyter

2. Forecast for 20xx sales in Eastern and Western Region — D. Rhyter

3. Recommendations for ways to reduce travel and meeting costs (Please bring your suggestions in writing for consideration by our travel and event planning managers.) — R. Manning

4. Sales presentation — J. Leblanc

5. Preliminary sales budgets for the upcoming year — H. Singh

APPOINTMENT

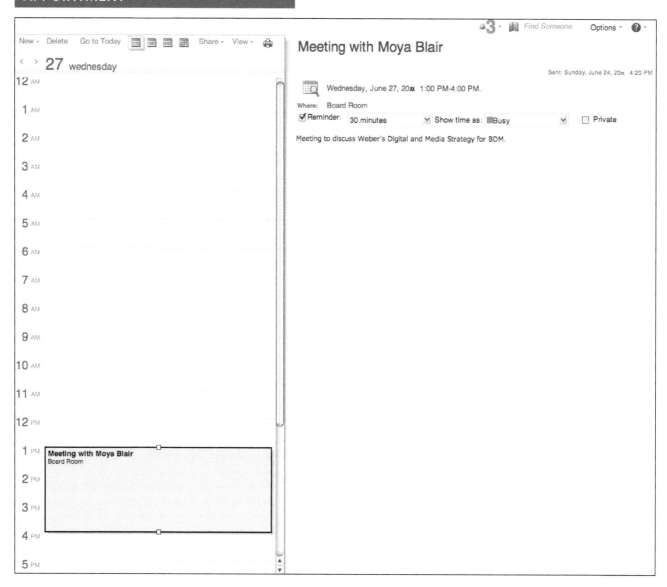

BIOGRAPHY

BIOGRAPHY

(Name)

Xxxxxxxxxxxxxxxxxxxxxxxxxxxxxxxxxxxxxxxxxxxxxxxxxxxxxxxxxxxxxxxxxxxxx
xxxxxxxxxxxxxxxxxxxxxxxxxxxxxxxxxxxxxxxxxxxxxxxxxxxxxxxxxxxxxxxxxxxxx
xxxxxxxxxxxxxxxxxxxxxxxxxxxxxxxxxxxxxxxxxxxxxxxxxxxxxxxxxxxxxxxxxxxxx
xxxxxxxxxxx.

Xxxxxxxxxxxxxxxxxxxxxxxxxxxxxxxxxxxxxxxxxxxxxxxxxxxxxxxxxxxxxxxxxxxxx
xxxxxxxxxxxxxxxxxxxxxxxxxxxxxxxxxxxxxxxxxxxxxxxxxxxxxxxxxxxxxxxxxxxxx
xxxxxxxxxxxxxxxxxxxxxxxxxxxxxxxxxxxxxxxxxxxxxxxxxxxxxxxxxxxxxxxxxxxxxxxxxx
xxxxxxxxxxxxxxxxxxxxxxxxxxxxxxxxxxxxxxxxx.

BUSINESS CARDS

Katelyn Kooy

Manager Finance

820 - 360 Albert Street
Ottawa, ON   K1R 7X7
613-237-9482, ext. 500
613-237-9400 (fax)
kooy@bdm.emp.ca

Keeping You in the Game
Berry, Duthie & Miller

Katelyn Kooy

Manager Finance

820 - 360 Albert Street
Ottawa, ON   K1R 7X7
613-237-9482, ext. 500
613-237-9400 (fax)
kooy@bdm.emp.ca

Keeping You in the Game
Berry, Duthie & Miller

Katelyn Kooy

Manager Finance

820 - 360 Albert Street
Ottawa, ON   K1R 7X7
613-237-9482, ext. 500
613-237-9400 (fax)
kooy@bdm.emp.ca

Keeping You in the Game
Berry, Duthie & Miller

Katelyn Kooy

Manager Finance

820 - 360 Albert Street
Ottawa, ON   K1R 7X7
613-237-9482, ext. 500
613-237-9400 (fax)
kooy@bdm.emp.ca

Keeping You in the Game
Berry, Duthie & Miller

Katelyn Kooy

Manager Finance

820 - 360 Albert Street
Ottawa, ON   K1R 7X7
613-237-9482, ext. 500
613-237-9400 (fax)
kooy@bdm.emp.ca

Keeping You in the Game
Berry, Duthie & Miller

Katelyn Kooy

Manager Finance

820 - 360 Albert Street
Ottawa, ON   K1R 7X7
613-237-9482, ext. 500
613-237-9400 (fax)
kooy@bdm.emp.ca

Keeping You in the Game
Berry, Duthie & Miller

Katelyn Kooy

Manager Finance

820 - 360 Albert Street
Ottawa, ON   K1R 7X7
613-237-9482, ext. 500
613-237-9400 (fax)
kooy@bdm.emp.ca

Keeping You in the Game
Berry, Duthie & Miller

Katelyn Kooy

Manager Finance

820 - 360 Albert Street
Ottawa, ON   K1R 7X7
613-237-9482, ext. 500
613-237-9400 (fax)
kooy@bdm.emp.ca

Keeping You in the Game
Berry, Duthie & Miller

CONTACT

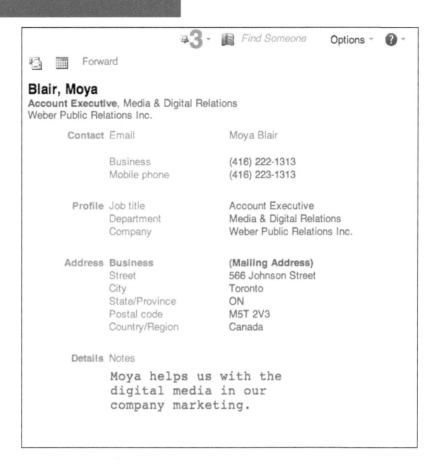

COVER LETTER (PROSPECTING)

YOUR NAME
YOUR MAILING ADDRESS
YOUR PHONE/CELL NUMBER
YOUR EMAIL

Date

Name of Contact
Organization Name
Organization Address
City, Province Postal Code

Dear Mr./Ms. (Last Name):

As a recently graduated Office Administrative Assistant, I am pleased to submit my application for a position at ABC Company Ltd. With my newly acquired skills, along with a background of hands-on experience in office administration, I am confident in my ability to become a central member of your organization.

In my educational and administratively related jobs, I have gained many skills in setting up staff events, creating and editing corporate-related documents, organizing travel, and setting up meetings. I am very self-directed and a conceptual team player. In addition, I have strong interpersonal and technical communication skills. My enclosed résumé provides more details about my specific clerical and administrative skills.

As an experienced and dedicated candidate, I welcome the chance to meet with you to discuss how my education, administrative experience, and skill set would be beneficial for ABC Company. I am available to meet with you at your convenience to further discuss my qualifications. I will call you next week to follow up.

Thank you for your time and consideration.

Sincerely,

(Signature)

[Typed Name]

Enclosure

820 - 360 Albert Street
Ottawa, ON K1R 7X7

info@bdm.emp.ca

613-237-9482 (telephone)
613-237-9400 (fax)

www.bdm.emp.ca

COVER LETTER (SOLICITED)

YOUR NAME
YOUR MAILING ADDRESS
YOUR PHONE/CELL NUMBER
YOUR EMAIL

Date

Name of Contact
Organization Name
Organization Address
City, Province Postal Code

Attention: (If applying to the Human Resources Department)

Dear Mr./Ms. (Last Name):

Subject: (If a certain Job No. or Application Code is required)

I am writing in response to your current job advertisement for an Administrative Assistant. Having my Office Administration Executive diploma and hands-on experience in general office administration, I am confident in my ability to become a central member of your organization.

In my educational and administratively related jobs, I have gained many skills: setting up staff events, creating and editing corporate-related documents, organizing travel, and organizing meetings. I am very self-directed and a team player. In addition, I have strong interpersonal and technical communication skills. My enclosed résumé provides more details about my specific clerical and administrative skills.

As an experienced and dedicated candidate, I welcome the chance to meet with you to discuss how my education, administrative experience, and skill set would be beneficial for this position. I am available to meet with you at your convenience to further discuss my qualifications. I will call you next week to follow up.

Thank you for your time and consideration.

Sincerely,

(Signature)

[Typed Name]

Enclosure

820 - 360 Albert Street
Ottawa, ON K1R 7X7

info@bdm.emp.ca

613-237-9482 (telephone)
613-237-9400 (fax)

www.bdm.emp.ca

EMAIL

To: duthie@bdm.emp.ca; miller@bdm.emp.ca

Subject: Budget Meeting

Good morning. I would like to meet next Monday at 10 a.m. to go over the draft budget. I have asked Cecil, our accountant, to be available should we have any questions.

If you have a schedule conflict, please let me know.

Lynn

Lynn Berry
President
Berry, Duthie & Miller

FAX COVER

Keeping You in the Game
Berry, Duthie & Miller

820 - 360 Albert Street
Ottawa, ON K1R 7X7

info@bdm.emp.ca

613-237-9482 (telephone)
613-237-9400 (fax)

www.bdm.emp.ca

FAX

To: Myles Berry

Fax No.: 613-727-7606

Date: September 7, 20xx

From: Lynn Berry

No. of pages (including cover page): 2

If pages are missing, please contact: Fiona Say, ext. 300

Comments:

Attached is an RFP for new course development. The deadline is September 30, 20xx, should you wish to participate.

ASSOCIATION OF INTERNATIONAL ADMINISTRATORS

Dunn University
Durham, NC USA 27708-04043
Tel: (919) 668-1927
Fax: (919) 684-8747
aiea@dunn.edu

September 7, 20xx

Ms. Catherine Jones
Manager of Training and Marketing
Global Business Institute
1500 – 99 Bank Street
Ottawa, ON K1P 6B9

Dear Ms. Jones:

Re: 20xx Conference in Vancouver

It is with great pleasure that I extend to you an invitation to attend our 20xx conference to be held this year at the Westin Bayshore in beautiful Vancouver, British Columbia from February 20 to 23, 20xx. The cost of the conference is $1,750, and the fee is payable by Friday, October 29, 20xx, by cheque payable to the Association of International Administrators.

This year's focus is upcoming training sessions in business. Since the Global Business Institute is one of Ottawa's leaders in this area, an overview of your upcoming new course offerings would be of value to our audience. Would you be able to present at this year's session? We have allowed a time slot of approximately ten minutes. This would be an excellent forum for marketing the Global Business Institute.

Please confirm your attendance and your decision to be a presenter by email to my assistant, Grace Hamilton, by Friday, October 1, 20xx. Her email address is ghamilton@dunn.edu.

A conference package will be forwarded to you by the end of December, and, should you consent to speak at this conference, Grace Hamilton will be contacting you for biographical information.

Sincerely,

ASSOCIATION OF INTERNATIONAL ADMINISTRATORS

Darla Dear

Dr. Darla Deer
Executive Director

> - *Are you available?*
> - *Are you attending?*
> - *Are you presenting?*
> - *I will confirm for you.*

INTEROFFICE MEMORANDUM

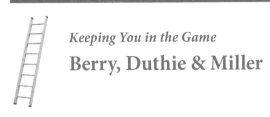

Keeping You in the Game

Berry, Duthie & Miller

INTEROFFICE MEMORANDUM

To: Fiona Say

From: Lynn Berry

Date: February 10, 20xx

Subject: Vacation Schedule

Would you please prepare an interoffice memorandum for my signature to the vice-presidents and directors requesting their plans for vacation for this year. We want to ensure that there is little overlap.

I would like this information by the end of February.

INTERVIEW QUESTION EXAMPLES

The Internet provides many examples of interview questions. Below is a sample of some commonly used questions in office administration. Review these and research more on the Internet:

- Tell me about yourself.

- What has been your favourite experience so far (volunteer or paid) and why?

- Why did you leave your last position?

- If I were to ask your last employer about your work ethic, what would he/she say?

- What do you know about our organization?

- Are you willing to travel or relocate?

- Can you give an example of a time when you were challenged ethically in your work or volunteer position? Explain that time. How did you handle it?

- Give me an example of a conflict you had with a colleague or superior in your work or volunteer position. Explain the conflict generally. How did you resolve the conflict?

- If you were to choose a word to describe yourself, what would it be and why?

- What was the most challenging work or volunteer position you have experienced and why?

- Why should I choose you as the best candidate for this position?

- In your opinion, what is the quality of your work?

- Why do you want to work for our organization?

JOB APPLICATION FORM

Instructions: Print clearly in black or blue ink. Answer all questions. Sign and date the form.

PERSONAL INFORMATION

First Name: _____

Middle Name: _____

Last Name: _____

Street Address: _____

_____

City, Province, Postal Code:

_____

Phone Number: (_____) _____

POSITION/AVAILABILITY

Position Applied For: _____

EDUCATION

Name and Address of School – Degree/Diploma – Graduation Date:

_____

_____

Skills and Qualifications (Licences, Skills, Training, Awards):

_____

_____

EMPLOYMENT HISTORY

Present or Previous Position

Employer: _____

Address: _____

Supervisor: _____

Phone Number: (_____) _____

Email: _____

Position Title: _____

JOB APPLICATION FORM (Page 2)

From: _____ To: _____

Responsibilities: _____

_____

Salary: _____

Reason for Leaving: _____

Previous Position

Employer: _____

Address: _____

Supervisor: _____

Phone Number: (_____) _____

Email: _____

Position Title: _____

From: _____ To: _____

Responsibilities: _____

_____

Salary: _____

Reason for Leaving: _____

May We Contact Your Present Employer?   Yes: _____   No: _____

References: (3)

Name/Title, Address, Phone:

_____

_____

_____

I certify that information contained in this application is true and complete. I understand that false information may be grounds for not hiring me or for immediate termination of employment at any point in the future if I am hired. I authorize the verification of any or all information listed above.

Signature: _____

JOB SEARCH TRACKING

Date: _____

COMPANY NAME (Applied To)	ADDRESS	TELEPHONE NO.	EMAIL	CONTACT NAME	DATE OF CONTACT	NOTES
XYZ Incorporated	123 ABC Lane Johnson, ON P1A 3V3	(705) 222-1222	johnjones@gmail.com	John Jones	February 3, 20xx	Contacted Mr. Jones and sent in my résumé. Will call XYZ in five business days to follow up.

LETTER

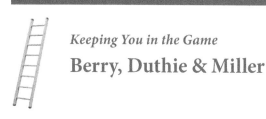

Keeping You in the Game

Berry, Duthie & Miller

September 7, 20xx

Mr. Eric Bingham
Director of Training
Global Business Centre
1500 - 80 Universal Avenue
Ottawa, ON K2G 3M6

Dear Mr. Bingham:

Subject: Upcoming Marketing Conference

It is with great pleasure that we invite you to our upcoming marketing conference scheduled for Friday, September 25, 20xx. The conference is scheduled from 1 to 4 p.m. in Conference Room A at our office.

We will be demonstrating 100 items from our new product line that will be valuable to your firm. Attached is our latest catalogue for your review.

Please confirm your attendance with our assistant, Fiona Say, by September 4, 20xx, at
613-237-9482, ext. 300. We look forward to meeting you.

Sincerely,

Blake Moore
Director of Marketing and Sales

Attachment

820 - 360 Albert Street
Ottawa, ON K1R 7X7

info@bdm.emp.ca

613-237-9482 (telephone)
613-237-9400 (fax)

www.bdm.emp.ca

OURTOWN COUNCIL MEETING

Minutes
June 3, 20xx
8:30 p.m.
Council Chambers

In Attendance

Mayor Oscar Maddison **(Chair)**
David Winter, Councillor
Iris Little, Councillor
Taylor Duncan, Councillor
Neil Berber, Councillor
Justin Medley **(Secretary)**

Absent with Regrets

Robert Thompson, Councillor
Tina Whitmore, Councillor

Absent

Henry Alcock, Councillor

Staff Members in Attendance

Sylvie Redmond, Clerk
Katy Benson, Secretary
Paul Hyres, Commissioner of Planning
Mariah Sutton, CEO Library Board

1. Call to Order

The meeting was called to order by Chair Oscar Maddison at 8:05 p.m.

2. Approval of Agenda

Iris Little MOVED that the agenda be approved. David Winter SECONDED the motion. The motion was APPROVED.

3. Approval of Previous Minutes

Neil Berber MOVED that the minutes of the meeting dated May 3, 20xx be approved. Taylor Duncan SECONDED the motion. The motion was APPROVED.

MINUTES – FORMAL STYLE (Page 2)

4. <u>Old Business</u>

The Welcome to Ourtown travel brochure was examined and approved for publishing.

Action: Taylor Duncan is to prepare the brochure for publishing.

5. <u>Reports</u>

a. Ourtown Library Board

David Winter MOVED that the recommendations of the Library Board be approved. Iris Little SECONDED the motion. The motion was APPROVED.

Action: Katy Benson to prepare a report for next meeting on the feasibility of imposing library fees.

b. Ourtown Recreation Association

Iris Little MOVED that the recommendations of the Recreation Association be approved. Neil Berber SECONDED the motion. The motion was APPROVED.

6. <u>Next Meeting</u>

The next meeting will be held in the Council Chambers at 8:30 p.m. on July 31, 20xx.

7. <u>Adjournment</u>

The Chair adjourned the meeting at 9:45 p.m.

Approved this _____ day of _____, 20xx

_____   _____
Chair – Mayor Oscar Maddison   Secretary – Justin Medley

EXECUTIVE INTEGRATED PROJECTS
CLASS MEETING

Minutes
January 14, 20xx
2 p.m.
Room B366

In Attendance

(Professor Name) **(Chair)**
(Student Names)

Absent with Regrets

(Student Name(s))

Absent

(Student Name(s))

1. Call to Order

The meeting was called to order by (Professor Name) at 2:05 p.m.

2. Approval of Agenda

(PROFESSOR NAME) MOVED that the agenda be approved. (STUDENT NAME) SECONDED the motion. The motion was APPROVED.

3. Approval of Minutes of Last Meeting

(PROFESSOR NAME) MOVED that the minutes be approved. (STUDENT NAME) SECONDED the motion. The motion was APPROVED.

4. Old Business

(Professor Name) recapped the history of Career Event and some of the ideas from previous classes.

5. Reports

a. Committee A

- Venue choices are being reviewed
- A/V Equipment must be considered in the venue choice.

b. Committee B

Coffee and donuts will be the food and beverage considered for the Career Event.

6. New Business

a. Convocation

- The location will be Mercury Hall.
- The date will be either June 18 or 19; this has not been announced yet.
- The Registrar's Office will send out invitations in spring.

b. Graduation Party

- Surveys have been distributed and summarized.
- The party is held in April after the last exam, typically.

   Action: (PROFESSOR NAME) to determine if first year students will attend. She is to report back next class.

c. Career Event Update

- Sign-up sheet will become available shortly.
- Each student should volunteer for at least one activity.
- Students can work in pairs.

   Action: (STUDENT NAME) to review student timetables to determine best date for event. She is to report back next week.

7. Next Meeting

The next meeting will be held in two weeks. Final dates and times will be emailed to all participants in the next few days.

8. Adjournment

The Chair adjourned the meeting at 3:45 p.m.

NOTICE OF MEETING

(Name of Meeting)

A meeting has been scheduled for (date, time, and location).

Please forward any agenda items to (name of person) by (date).

Should you not be able to attend, please let (name of person) know as soon as possible.

Distribution:

(Names)

NOTICE OF MEETING (INTERNAL) BY EMAIL

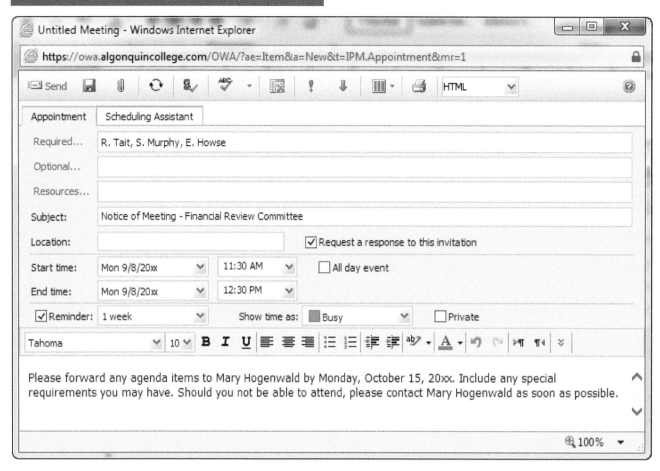

NOTICE OF MEETING (EXTERNAL) BY EMAIL

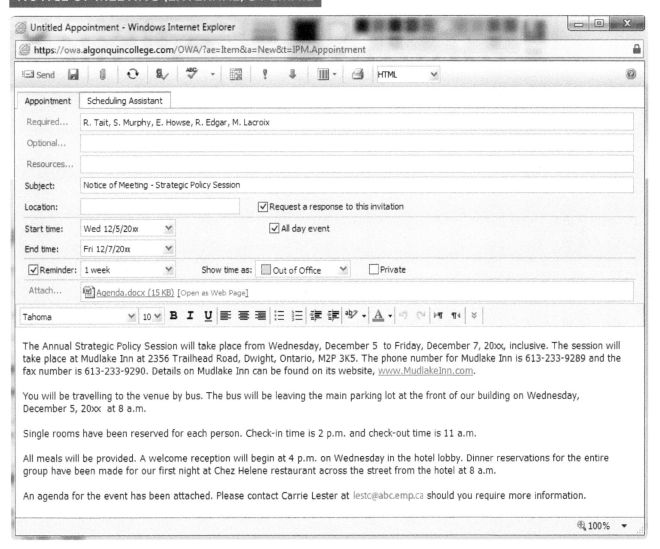

The Annual Strategic Policy Session will take place from Wednesday, December 5 to Friday, December 7, 20xx, inclusive. The session will take place at Mudlake Inn at 2356 Trailhead Road, Dwight, Ontario, M2P 3K5. The phone number for Mudlake Inn is 613-233-9289 and the fax number is 613-233-9290. Details on Mudlake Inn can be found on its website, www.MudlakeInn.com.

You will be travelling to the venue by bus. The bus will be leaving the main parking lot at the front of our building on Wednesday, December 5, 20xx at 8 a.m.

Single rooms have been reserved for each person. Check-in time is 2 p.m. and check-out time is 11 a.m.

All meals will be provided. A welcome reception will begin at 4 p.m. on Wednesday in the hotel lobby. Dinner reservations for the entire group have been made for our first night at Chez Helene restaurant across the street from the hotel at 8 a.m.

An agenda for the event has been attached. Please contact Carrie Lester at lestc@abc.emp.ca should you require more information.

POST-INTERVIEW JOB SEARCH TRACKING

Date: _____

COMPANY NAME (Applied To)	ADDRESS	TELEPHONE NO.	EMAIL	CONTACT NAME	DATE OF CONTACT	NOTES
XYZ Incorporated	123 ABC Lane Johnson, ON P1A 3V3	(705) 222-1222	johnjones@gmail.com	John Jones	February 3, 20xx	Contacted Mr. Jones and sent in my résumé. Will call XYZ in five business days to follow up.
XYZ Incorporated POST-INTERVIEW NOTES:						

PROJECTION TABLE USING AN ABSOLUTE CELL REFERENCE

PROJECTED STUDENT GROWTH			
Year	Number of Students	Increase	Projected Number of Students
20xx	53.00	1.06	54.06
20xx	54.06	1.08	55.14
20xx	55.14	1.10	56.24
20xx	56.24	1.12	57.37
20xx	57.37	1.15	58.52
Increase		2%	

PROJECTED STUDENT GROWTH		
Year	Number of Students	Projected Number of Students
20xx	53	=B6*B11
20xx	54	=B7*B11
20xx	55	=B8*B11
20xx	56	=B9*B11
20xx	57	=B10*B11
Increase	2%	

REQUEST FOR PROPOSAL (Page 1)

Berry, Duthie & Miller

REQUEST FOR PROPOSAL

Submission Requirements

Submission Due Date	February 15, 20xx	Time	12 noon
Submission Method	by fax		

Contact Information

General			
Company/Organization Name	The Office Supply Company		
Address 1	1022 Bank Street		
Address 2			
City	Ottawa	Province	Ontario
Postal Code	K1A 0T9		
Contact Person			
Salutation	Mr.		
Last Name	Wilde	First Name	O.
Phone	613-234-1111	Fax	613-234-0011
Email Address	wildeo@osc.emp.ca		

Facility Information

General			
Name	Conference Centre		
Address	1234 Colonnade Road		
City	Ottawa	Province	Ontario
Postal Code	K2L 3K2	Phone	613-724-4101
Fax Number	613-724-4110	Email	info@ccentre.emp.ca
Web Address	www.ccentre.emp.ca		

REQUEST FOR PROPOSAL (Page 2)

General Meeting Requirements

Meeting Name	Annual Sales Meeting		
Dates			
Function Start Date	May 20, 20xx	Function End Date	May 23, 20xx
Alternate Start Date	May 19, 20xx	Alternate End Date	May 22, 20xx
Arrival Date	May 19, 20xx	Departure Date	May 24, 20xx
Alternate Arrival Date	May 18, 20xx	Alternate Departure Date	May 23, 20xx
Number of People	15		
Notes	One participating on the first day (i.e., May 20) only and will not be staying overnight		

Meeting Room(s)

General			
Start Date	May 20, 20xx	End Date	May 23, 20xx
Capacity		Setup Type	
Equipment and Furniture			
☐ Chairs	☐ Tables	☐ Microphone	
☐ Projector	☐ Videotaping	☐ Wireless Internet Access	
☐ Screen	☐ Video Projector		
Other (Specify)			
Services			
☐ Setup	☐ Cleanup	☐ Other	

Accommodations

Check-in Time		Check-out Time	
Single Number Required	14	Cost per night	
Double Number Required		Cost per night	
Suite Number Required		Cost per night	

REQUEST FOR PROPOSAL (Page 3)

Amenities

☐ Business Services	☐ Fitness Centre	☐ Golf
☐ High Speed Internet	☐ Indoor Pool	☐ Outdoor Pool
☐ Parking		
Other		

Food and Beverage

Type	Required	Cost of each	Description/Notes (i.e., if event is +1 day, indicate dates required)
Breakfast	☒	$	May 20–24, inclusive
Lunch	☒	$	May 20–23, inclusive
Reception	☒	$	May 19
Dinner	☒	$	May 20–23, inclusive
Breaks	☒	$	May 20–23, inclusive

RÉSUMÉ – CHRONOLOGICAL (Page 1)

YOUR NAME
YOUR MAILING ADDRESS
YOUR PHONE NUMBER/CELL NUMBER
YOUR EMAIL ADDRESS

OBJECTIVE (Optional)

The Objective section is often used to help the employer or recipient of this résumé focus on your strengths. Remember that your strengths should match those required for the position that is open.

Example:
A challenging position as an administrative assistant, which demands excellent professional, technical, and interpersonal skills.

EDUCATION

Provide a list of all education, including the name of the institution, dates, and certificates or diplomas received. Do not use high school unless you are just beginning your post-secondary years. If you do not have a lot of experience or education beyond your high school years, you may want to also include those years of education.

Example:
20xx   Algonquin College, Ottawa, ON
*   Graduate of Office Administration—Executive Diploma*

WORK EXPERIENCE

List your experience based on years starting with the most recent and working back. You should list the start and end date including month and year, name of organization, location, and a brief description of your duties.

Example:
Summer 20xx   Department of Justice, Government of Canada (Student Term)
*   Assisted with photocopying, data entry, switchboard, and keyboarding correspondences*

VOLUNTEER EXPERIENCE

Volunteer experience is just as important as paid work experience. You may wish to combine the Work Experience and Volunteer Experience sections if your paid positions are smaller in number than your volunteer positions. List the start and end dates including month and year, the name of the organization, and a brief description of the position.

Example:
Summer 20xx   Assistant Coach, Johnson Valley Soccer Team
*   Worked with a Pee Wee level soccer team developing skills, consistency, and dedication to the sport of soccer.*

RÉSUMÉ – CHRONOLOGICAL (Page 2)

INTERESTS

If you have room on your résumé, you may want to include your interests outside of working (volunteer or paid). This list can be anything from reading to travelling to exercise. Your list of interests will help the employer to see you as a well-rounded person with balance in your life, and will also serve as icebreakers during the interview process.

Example:
Reading, Writing Poetry, Downhill Skiing, Hiking, Travelling, Camping

REFERENCES

If there is room on your résumé, you may list your references. Have three or four on your list. If there is not room, you can simply state: *References Available Upon Request.* It is imperative that you have received confirmation from the references and that you have an up-to-date address, phone number, and email address for each one.

Example:
Mr. John Jones, Manager
Stedman's Department Store
Johnson Valley, ON P2P 0H0
(613) 222-1112

Note: Remember to label Page 2, if your résumé includes two pages.

Example:
Page 2   *Joan Masterson*

YOUR NAME
YOUR MAILING ADDRESS
YOUR PHONE NUMBER/CELL NUMBER
YOUR EMAIL ADDRESS

OBJECTIVE (Optional)

The Objective section is often used to help the employer or recipient of this résumé focus on your strengths. Remember that your strengths should match those required for the position that is open.

Example:
To gain a position, as an administrative assistant, that showcases my present skills and challenges me in new and exciting ways.

EDUCATION

Provide a list of all education and educational institutions. If you have had gaps in your education, consider omitting the dates. Dates may only emphasize years where you were not moving forward in education or work.

Example:
20xx   Algonquin College, Ottawa, ON
*   Graduate of Office Administration—Executive Diploma*

Note: Dates should be used in the education area because your education is the most up-to-date skill you have, upon taking this course.

SKILLS

The skills list should highlight those skills you wish to emphasize for your future employer. The Work Experience and Volunteer Experience sections below can explain the context in which those skills were obtained.

Example:

Goal-Oriented	*Self-Directed and Positive Team Player*	*Efficient (Time Management Skills)*
Conceptual	*Strong Interpersonal Skills*	*Passion for Learning*

WORK EXPERIENCE

List your experience based on the examples of experience you wish to share. Each experience should have a brief description of the types of skills you acquired. Dates are not necessary.

Example:
Valleyview Department Store
Retail position involving customer service, troubleshooting customer complaints, stocking shelves, cleaning, merchandising, assisting in creating display windows, and balancing cash.

RÉSUMÉ – FUNCTIONAL (Page 2)

VOLUNTEER EXPERIENCE

Volunteer experience is just as important as paid work experience. You may wish to combine the Work Experience and Volunteer Experience sections if your paid positions are smaller in number than your volunteer positions. List the organizations and include a brief description of each volunteer position.

Example:
Team Leader, Safe Neighbourhood
Organized a Safe Neighbourhood branch in the community. Team Leader position included monthly meetings, semi-annual reports to the national organization, and constant communication and open-door availability to the neighbourhood community in order to create an efficient and effective Safe Neighbourhood program.

INTERESTS

If you have room on your résumé, you may want to include your interests outside of working (volunteer or paid). This list can be anything from reading to travelling to exercise. Your list of interests will help the employer to see you as a well-rounded person with balance in your life, and will also serve as icebreakers during the interview process.

Example:
Reading, Writing Poetry, Downhill Skiing, Hiking, Travelling, Camping

REFERENCES

If there is room on your résumé, you may list your references. Have three or four on your list. If there is not room, you can simply state: *References Available Upon Request.* It is imperative that you have received confirmation from the references and that you have an up-to-date address, phone number, and email address for each one.

Example:
Mr. John Jones, Manager
Stedman's Department Store
Johnson Valley, ON   P2P 0H0
(613) 222-1112

Note: Remember to label Page 2 if your résumé includes two pages.

Example:
Page 2   *Joan Masterson*

SURVEY – PAPER FORMAT (Page 1)

Thank you for attending!

Please take a moment to answer the following questions in order to help us improve on next year's forum.

Please rate each of the following from 1 to 5, with 1 being the lowest and 5 being the highest.

---

1. What was your overall impression of Career Forum 20xx?

    1   2   3   4   5

2. How did you hear about Career Forum 20xx?

☐ Flyer   ☐ Another Student
☐ Teacher   ☐ Office Administration Forum

3. What is your class section?

☐ 010   ☐ Executive
☐ 020   ☐ Legal
☐ 030   ☐ Double Diploma

4. Please rate the following facilities:

	1	2	3	4	5
Room Location	1	2	3	4	5
Room Temperature	1	2	3	4	5
Seating	1	2	3	4	5
Refreshments	1	2	3	4	5
Audio Equipment	1	2	3	4	5

5. Please rate each of the following panelists:

	1	2	3	4	5
Public Service Commission	1	2	3	4	5
Employment Services	1	2	3	4	5
IAAP	1	2	3	4	5
Employment Agency	1	2	3	4	5
Former Legal Graduate	1	2	3	4	5
Former Executive Graduate	1	2	3	4	5
Image Consultant	1	2	3	4	5
Interviewer	1	2	3	4	5

SURVEY – PAPER FORMAT (Page 2)

6. How useful was the information that each of the panelists provided?

       1   2   3   4   5

7. What did you enjoy the most?

8. Would you recommend Career Forum 20xx to future students?

    ☐ YES   ☐ NO

    If not, why not?

9. What would you have done differently?

Thank you for your participation, suggestions, and comments!
April 20xx

TASK

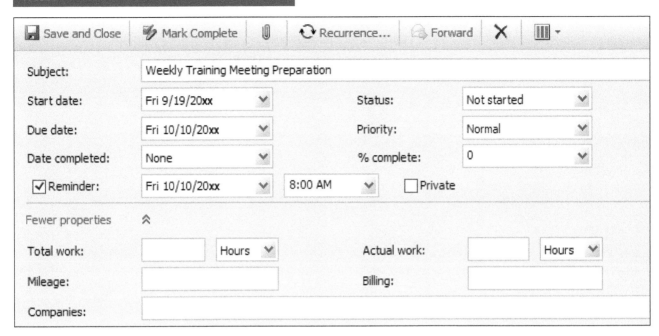

THANK-YOU LETTER

YOUR NAME
YOUR MAILING ADDRESS
YOUR PHONE NUMBER/CELL NUMBER
YOUR EMAIL ADDRESS

Today's Date

Name of Interviewer
Organization Name
Organization Address
City, Province Postal Code

Dear Mr./Ms. (Last Name):

Thank you so much for the opportunity to meet with you to discuss the position of (Position) on Thursday, February xx, 20xx. I thoroughly enjoyed my tour of the company and the insight I now have into your organization.

My education and administrative-related positions have equipped me with many tools to meet the tight deadlines and high energy required for the day-to-day duties. I would be excited to meet the challenges of (Name of Company).

Thank you, once again, for your time and consideration. I would be happy to answer any further questions, should they arise.

Sincerely,

(Signature)

[Typed Name]

TRAVEL AUTHORIZATION

Berry, Duthie & Miller

Travel Authorization

General Information

Name: Blake Moore	Employee No.: 21244
Position: Director	Department: Marketing and Sales

Party to Visit: Teleglobe Canada
Location: Vancouver, British Columbia
Purpose of Trip: Video Conferencing Seminar

From: September 1, 20xx	To: September 3, 20xx

Estimated Cost

Account No.	Cost Centre	Location	Amount
3100-09	5200	Vancouver	$5,000

Transportation

Air: ☒ Yes ☐ No	Rail: ☐ Yes ☒ No	Car: ☒ Yes ☐ No Avis Car Rental	Other:

Describe:
Ottawa–Vancouver–Ottawa

Accommodation

Required: ☒ Yes ☐ No	Number of Nights: 2	From: September 1, 20xx	To: September 3, 20xx
Preferred:	(1) Holiday Inn Downtown	(2)	(3)

Travel Advance

Date Required: August 25, 20xx	Canadian	U.S.	Other
Cash (Max $150)			
Company Cheque	$550		
Travellers' Cheques			
Total Advance	$550		
Foreign Exchange			
Canadian Equivalent			

Authorization

Employee Signature: *Blake Moore*	Date: August 18, 20xx	Authorized By:	Date:

TRAVEL EXPENSE CLAIM (Page 1)

BERRY, DUTHIE & MILLER TRAVEL EXPENSE CLAIM

CLAIMANT	Employee No.	Party visited
Lynn Berry	24677	Association of Canadian Educators

Purpose of trip	Date of claim	Lcn/city **Halifax**
Educators' Annual Conference	05/10/20xx	Province **Nova Scotia**

For period from: 10/09/20xx to 15/09/20xx inclusive   Country **Canada**

EXPENSES PAID BY CLAIMANT

					HST	TOTALS
1	Claimant's auto	30 km @	$0.45 /km)			13.50
	(itemize on sheet 2)					

2 Other transportation

Date	Carrier	Ticket No.	Amount		
9-Sep	Blue Line	B877	15.00		
					15.00

3 Accommodation

Date	City	Hotel/Motel	Amount		

		TOTALS
4	Meals and related gratuities (itemize on sheet 2)	139.00
5	Other expenses (itemize on sheet 2)	15.00
6	Total expenses paid by claimant	**$182.50**
7	Deduct cash advance(s)	(300.00)
8	Balance owed to:	
	Claimant ☐ Company ☒	**$117.50**

EXPENSES CHARGED TO BDM — Amount

Date	Description	Ticket No.	Canada	Outside
2-Sep	Airfare	AC8766	800.99	
14-Sep	Delta Inn (10-14 Sep)	18899	500.00	
12-Sep	Hard Rock Café		130.00	
2-Sep	Conference Fee		500.00	
9	Total Expenses Charged to BDM		**$1,930.00**	

TOTAL EXPENSES (line 6 plus 9)

Acc't No.	Cost Centre	Location	Amount	Accounting Use Only
12345	5900	HFX	$2,112.50	
				T.V. Number
				Claim Number
				TAX (Meals)

Claimant: I hereby certify that this claim is correct in all respects and in accordance with company policy, and that expenses claimed were actually incurred on BDM business.

	TOTAL	**$2,112.50**
	Recommended	Date

Signature

Date | Approved | Date

Send original to Travel (attach receipts, ticket stubs, etc. as required by Policy 5.14)

TRAVEL EXPENSE CLAIM (Page 2)

	SPENT IN CANADA						SPENT OUTSIDE CANADA				
	MEAL EXPENSES						MEAL EXPENSES				
Date	Location	B'kfast	Lunch	Dinner	TOTAL	Date	Location	B'kfast	Lunch	Dinner	TOTAL
10-Sep	HFX			25.00	25.00						
11-Sep	HFX	8.00	6.00	16.00	30.00						
12-Sep	HFX	4.00	6.00	20.00	30.00						
13-Sep	HFX	8.00	9.00		17.00						
14-Sep	HFX	8.00	5.50	16.50	30.00						
15-Sep	HFX	7.00			7.00						

| HST | | TOTAL to line 4 sheet 1 | **139.00** | | | HST | | TOTAL to line 4 sheet 1 | |

Date	Description of other expenses (in Canada)	Km (line 1)	Other (line 5)	Date	Description of other expenses (outside Canada)	Other (line 5)
14-Sep	Tips		15.00			
14-Sep	Mileage from Airport	30 km				

| HST | | TOTAL | 15.00 | | | TOTAL | |

sheet 2   Record all expenses in Canadian funds. Do not extract HST from receipts.

TRAVEL EXPENSES TABLE

TRAVEL EXPENSES

Expense	Canadian (CAD)	Foreign (GBP)	Converted
Flight	3,000.00		3,000.00
Hotel		400.00	725.17
Conference	1,500.00		1,500.00
Ground (Canada)	70.00		70.00
Ground (Destination)		40.00	70.00
Miscellaneous	100.00		100.00
Meals	200.00		200.00
Total			*5,665.17

* Round to $5,700.00

ITINERARY FOR NATHAN BLACK

Vancouver, British Columbia
September 4 to September 11, 20xx

Monday, September 4

1030   Blue Line taxi arranged for transportation to airport from your home

1300   Depart Macdonald-Cartier International Airport, AC 442

        (No food is served on the flight; however, food can be purchased using cash or credit card on board)

1525   Arrive Vancouver International Airport (Note that this is 1825 in Ottawa)

1630   Free Shuttle to Hilton Downtown (find shuttle at Gate Post 312 outside main doors of airport)

        Hilton Downtown
        Street Address
        Telephone number
        Fax
        Email

        Guaranteed late arrival; reservation no. 22FTG for single occupancy room

        Requests: near fire escape and away from elevator

Tuesday, September 5

0625   Breakfast meeting with John Saunders

        John's title
        Company name
        Company address
        Company phone number
        Topic of meeting

1100   No appointments or activities scheduled for this day

Wednesday, September 6

0900   National Sales Conference, National Training and Education Association
        Hilton Grand Ballroom

1200   Lunch (personal choice)

1600   Reception, Hilton Inn Lobby

1830   Conference Dinner, Hilton Inn Dining Room

TRAVEL ITINERARY – DOMESTIC (Page 2)

<u>Thursday, September 7</u>

0830   Depart Hilton Inn by free shuttle (shuttle has been pre-booked and driver will be waiting in front of the lobby doors) for Vancouver International Airport

1145   Depart Vancouver International Airport
AC 868

(No food is served on the flight; however, food can be purchased using cash or credit card on board)

2005   Arrive Macdonald-Cartier International Airport in Ottawa (Note that this is 1705 in Vancouver)

Blue Line taxi home

TRAVEL ITINERARY – INTERNATIONAL (Page 1)

ITINERARY FOR BLAKE MOORE

Berkshire, United Kingdom
September 4 to September 11, 20xx

Saturday, September 4

1230   Blue Line taxi arranged to pick you up at BDM outside front doors

1500   Depart Macdonald-Cartier International Airport in Ottawa
        AC 167

        (Drink and snack provided on board)

1600   Arrive Pearson International Airport in Toronto

1800   Depart Pearson International Airport in Toronto for London, UK
        AC 856

        (Supper and breakfast provided on board)

Sunday, September 5

0625   Arrive Heathrow International Airport in London, UK (Note that this is 0125 in Ottawa)

        Take reserved limousine (driver will be waiting for you at Post 322 outside Terminal 2 entrance) to
        hotel in Berkshire, UK

        Hilton Inn
        Street address
        Telephone number
        Fax
        Email

        Guaranteed late arrival, confirmation no. 1211 with Loretta, single room

        Requests: away from elevator

1200   No appointments or activities scheduled for this day

Monday, September 6 to Friday, September 10, 20xx

0900   Product Demonstration in the Hilton Inn Ballroom

1600   Reception, Hilton Inn Lobby

1630   Dinner, Hilton Inn Dining Room

TRAVEL ITINERARY – INTERNATIONAL (Page 2)

Saturday, September 11

0805	Depart Hilton Inn by limousine (driver will be waiting for you in the hotel lobby) for Heathrow International Airport
1105	Depart Heathrow International Airport for Toronto AC 863
1405	Arrive Pearson International Airport in Toronto (note that this is 1905 p.m. London time)
1605	Depart Pearson International Airport in Toronto for Ottawa AC 168
1700	Arrive Macdonald-Cartier International Airport in Ottawa
	Go to Gate 32 outside of main doors of airport and locate Blue Line taxi

Keeping You in the Game

Berry, Duthie & Miller

VOICE MESSAGE

To: Lynn Berry

From: Susan Halpert

Time: 9:50 a.m.

Date: September 7, 20xx

Subject: Fundraiser

Message:

Good morning, Lynn. We are organizing a fundraiser for a new women's shelter. We are hoping to break ground early next year; however, we are still short of start-up funding.

Since Berry, Duthie & Miller is so active in the community, I am hoping your company might be able to assist us with a donation. We would dedicate one of our training rooms for preparing the women for re-entry into the workplace to your company.

I can be reached at 613-555-5555. I look forward to discussing this exciting venture with you. Please call me at your earliest convenience.

Appendix E

Procedural Guide – Background Notes and Instructions

AGENDAS

An agenda, also referred to as an Order of Business, represents a list of topics to be discussed during a meeting. The document helps participants to prepare before and stay focused during the meeting. The agenda's content is based on the response to the notice.

The administrative assistant is responsible for keying, copying, and distributing the agenda. While preparing the document, the following must be kept in mind:

- Meeting start and end time, agenda items, and the name of the person responsible for each topic are included.
- Topics submitted relate to the goal of the meeting (if any are not related, the contributor should be contacted).
- The items are arranged in order of the topics to be discussed.
- An appropriate amount of time is allocated to the meeting. People expect that the meeting will end at the specified time.
- Breaks should be included if the meeting is long.
- The agenda should be prepared and sent to the participants as soon as possible to allow attendees sufficient time to prepare.

The structure of the agenda should match the style of the event (i.e., informal or formal). If informal, the agenda could be an email message or an attachment to an email message with the items to be discussed in a numbered list.

If the meeting is formal, the agenda should reflect the structure of a formal meeting and will include some or all of the following items:

- Call to Order
- Approval of the Agenda
- Approval of the Previous Meeting Minutes (additions, deletions, amendments)
- Old Business (from previous minutes)
- Reports
- New Business
- Date of the Next Meeting
- Adjournment

APPLYING ONLINE

Online Job Applications

You can post your résumé with ease using the Internet and by completing an online job application. Applications can be made online via a job board, like workopolis.com, or you can directly apply online to an organization's website.

You often have to register and build an applicant profile before you can apply online. Once you create a profile, you can apply for jobs online and set up search agents to email you when any new job posts are added to the system. Once jobs are up, you can apply with ease. Many job sites also give you a tracking system to record what jobs you have applied for.

Job Application Systems

Some online sites allow you to upload your own résumé, while others ask you to copy and paste your résumé into a résumé builder that is part of the site. Once you have uploaded your résumé, you will be able to search any job that is of interest to you. Be aware that some uploads will completely take the formatting out of your résumé, and it will not appear in the same way that you would present a résumé.

Company Websites

If you are interested in working for a particular company, go to the company website. Career information is usually listed in the "Careers" or the "About Us" section of the site. Follow the instructions for searching for and applying to jobs online.

Tools to Apply Online

When you apply online using an online application system, the system often will ask for your contact information, educational background, and employment history. You will need to have available the following information: Where did you work? When did you work there? What was your job title? What were you paid at your previous job?

Download a sample job application form and complete it before you start your online application. You will have all the information you need, ready to enter.

Online Employment Tests

Depending on the company, you may need to take—and pass—an online test to be considered for employment. Pre-employment tests are used to help an employer identify candidates who will be a good fit in the organization.

APPOINTMENTS

Internal

Record:

- Date
- Time
- Location (only if not in boss's office)
- Subject
- Telephone number (only if someone from outside the company has an appointment)

External

Record:

- Date
- Time
- Subject
- Location
- Address
- Room number
- Telephone number

BUSINESS CARDS

Creating a Single Business Card or a Single Sheet of Business Cards Using MS Word

1. In Word 2007 or later, choose Labels from the Mailings tab.

2. On the Labels tab, click **Options**.

3. In the Labels Product list, click **Avery Standard**.

4. In the Product Number list, click the type of Avery label you are using, such as 5371, 5372, 5376, or 5377 and click **OK**.

5. In the Address area, enter the address information for the business card.

   Note: To modify the formatting of the address, select the address, click the right mouse button (Windows) or hold down CONTROL and click the mouse (Mac), and then click **Font** or click **Paragraph** on the shortcut menu. Make the appropriate changes in the Font or Paragraph dialog boxes, and then click **OK**.

Printing a Single Business Card

To print a single business card at a specific location on the sheet of labels, follow these steps in the Envelopes and Labels dialog box:

1. Under Print, click **Single Label**.

2. Type the row and column for the print location of the card on the sheet of labels.

3. Click **Print**.

Printing an Entire Sheet of Business Cards

To print an entire sheet of the same business card, follow these steps in the Envelopes and Labels dialog box:

1. Under Print, click **Full page of the same label**.

2. Click **Print**.

To manually edit each card on the sheet, click **New Document**. Word creates a new document containing a sheet of business cards that you can edit before printing. You may also want to save the document as a template.

COVER LETTERS

Cover letters are created to help an employer learn enough about you to want to read on to the résumé. There are two kinds of cover letters:

- The Prospecting Cover Letter is used when asking about potential job opportunities with an employer. The applicant does not know whether there is a position but wants to work for this organization. A Prospecting Cover Letter should be about working for the organization, not necessarily working for a specific position.

- The Soliciting Cover Letter is used to apply for a specific position with a potential employer. The applicant knows there is a position through a newspaper or magazine advertisement, a job search website, company social media, or word of mouth. A Soliciting Cover Letter should be about the specific position and why your skills are perfect for that position. In addition, addressing where you heard about the job opportunity is important.

Include an attention line if you want to address a certain person within a department.

Subject lines are used to quote a specific job reference number or the title of the position.

Letters should be no more than four paragraphs. It is most common to use Full Block style, although Modified Block may also be used.

The way you set up your name, address, phone number, and email should be mirrored in your cover letter. Font style, font size, and paper quality should be the same for all components of the job search.

DOCUMENT TRACKING

Track Changes, the document tracking feature in Word, allows two or more individuals to collaborate on a document. The feature highlights modifications made by each person by displaying their changes in a unique colour. The types of changes tracked include additions, deletions, and formatting changes.

Comments can be added by each person and appear in the colour associated with that individual. Comments can be used to ask questions or provide additional information.

Tracking Changes

- Select the **Review** tab.
- Click the **Track Changes** button in the Tracking group.
- Begin changing the document by adding, deleting, and modifying the text; changes will appear as coloured markups.

Adding Comments

- Select text or position the cursor in the document where a comment is desired.
- Select the **Review** tab.
- Click **New Comment**.
- Key the text of the comment.

Viewing Changes

The edited document can be viewed using **Track Changes** in a variety of ways. For example, the versions (original or final) can be viewed with or without specific changes displayed. To change the view:

- Select the **Review** tab.
- Select **Track Changes**.
- Click the drop-down arrow beside **All Markup**.

Navigating to Changes

Changes made while tracking is turned on are considered suggestions. If they are to be permanent, the changes need to be accepted. First, you need to navigate to the change. To do this,

- Select the **Review** tab.
- Click the **Previous** or **Next** button in the Changes group.

Accepting or Rejecting Revisions

- Select the **Review** tab.
- Using the navigation buttons as described above, move to the first change.
- Accept or reject the change by clicking the **Accept** or **Reject** button in the Changes group; you will automatically advance to the next change, which can either be accepted or rejected.
- Save the file.

EDITING A MERGE

Recipient Lists (Data File)

- Select the **Mailings** tab.
- Click the **Select Recipients** button.
- Click **Use Existing List**; a file dialog box is displayed.
- Navigate to the file in which the list has been saved.
- Select the file and click **Open**.
- Click **Edit Recipient List**; a Mail Merge Recipient dialog box appears.
- Under Data Source, select the name of the file to activate the **Edit** button.
- Click **Edit**; the Edit Data Source dialog box appears.
- To add a new record, click the **New Entry** button.
- To delete an existing record, click the row representing the record and click **Delete Entry**.
- Once you are finished editing the recipient list, click **OK**.

Editing a Form Letter (Merge Fields)

- Open the form letter as you would any other Word document.
- Make the necessary changes; for example, you could merge the letter with a different recipient list by clicking **Select Recipients** in the Start Mail Merge group of Mailings.
- Save the letter.
- Preview the letter merged with the recipient list by clicking **Preview Results**; use the navigation buttons to move from one letter to the next.
- Merge the edited letter with the recipient list by clicking the **Edit Individual Letters** command in the Finish & Merge menu.
- Save and print the merged letters.

EXTERNAL MEETINGS (Page 1)

External meetings are held away from the office or place of business. This type of meeting may be selected because it provides:

- A location that is convenient for all participants who may be coming from different areas
- An environment free from distraction

The following outlines the basic steps in arranging an external meeting.

1. Prepare Initial Plan

- Determine the purpose of the meeting.
- Identify activities (in addition to the meeting, other activities such as workshops may be planned and guest speakers invited).
- Identify participants and potential guest speakers.
- Establish date(s).
- Prepare and distribute the notice of meeting to the participants.
- Determine the equipment (projector and screen, computer, etc.) required and ensure that it is available.
- Establish the budget (expenses may include transportation to and from the venue, rental of the venue, and refreshments).

2. Identify Location for External Meeting

The following checklist can serve as a guideline for identifying potential sites. Requests for Proposal (RFPs) may be used to identify the best location.

Location

- Distance to the facility
- Accessibility to the facility

Meeting Room

- Number of meeting rooms
- Size and shape of room
- Setup options
- Seating capacity (i.e., number of chairs and tables)
- General appearance
- Audiovisual equipment (projector and screen, microphones, PA system, etc.)
- Setup and cleanup services provided
- Business services available: faxing, telecommunications, or copying
- Refreshment options

EXTERNAL MEETINGS (Page 2)

Accommodations

- Number of rooms available and their type: double, single, twin
- Room amenities (Internet access, television, desk, and phone)
- Proximity to meeting facilities
- Business services (Internet, fax, copy, and print) available
- Parking availability
- Recreational facilities (e.g., pool and fitness centre)

3. Execute the Plan

- Contact the guest speaker(s); prepare and send correspondence to confirm attendance.
- Prepare and distribute the agenda and information to the participants including:
    - Location of meeting (include address, maps, and website address)
    - Transportation options to and from the meeting
    - Details regarding the hotel (e.g., check-in and check-out times)
    - Scheduled events including social activities

4. Anticipate and Manage Contingencies

- Immediately before the meeting, confirm arrangements with the contact person at the site (e.g., hotel, conference centre) regarding:
    - Meeting room and equipment
    - Selected menu
    - Accommodations
    - Total cost
- Arrive early to ensure that the meeting room is properly set up.
- Take minutes of the meeting(s).

5. Perform Post-Meeting Tasks

- Prepare and distribute minutes.
- Ensure that bills are paid.
- Prepare the financial report.
- Write letters of appreciation to the guest speaker(s).

FORMAL MEETINGS (Page 1)

Formal meetings should follow strict rules of order (see below). These rules are necessary to ensure that board, corporate, and committee meetings address necessary requirements (i.e., guarantee legality, follow agreed upon principles, etc.).

Sample Order of Business for Formal Meeting

1. Title (include the name of the organization, purpose of the meeting, date, time, location)

2. Call to Order

3. Approval of Agenda

4. Approval of Previous Meeting Minutes

5. Old Business

6. Reports

7. New Business

8. Date of Next Meeting

9. Adjournment

Robert's Rules of Order

These are a set of rules and procedures to assure order and resolve differences during a meeting. These rules are based on the procedures of the British Parliament. The following are some of the key terms used:

Quorum

The number of voting members that must be present at a meeting (according to the association's by-laws) in order to legally conduct business.

Order of Business

Agenda

Call to Order

Commence the meeting.

Motion

The motion is a proposal to be debated and for which a decision is required.

- The following is an example of a motion: "A motion was made by (name of person) and seconded by (name of person) that: Verbatim text of motion."
- The chairperson then repeats the motion. "It has been moved and seconded that . . ."

FORMAL MEETINGS (Page 2)

- Debate on the topic then occurs.
- When the debate finishes, voting occurs.
- The chairperson then says, "It has been resolved that . . ."

Voting

- Silent (ballot)
- Show of hands
- Voices (aye [yes], nay [no])

Resolution

This is a decision; it occurs when a motion has been voted upon and passed: "It has been resolved that . . ."

Amendment

- A proposed change to the original motion; this must be moved and seconded.
- Debate occurs around the amended motion and then is voted upon to replace the previous motion.

Point of Order

There is an irregularity in the proceedings of a meeting – e.g., a motion is irrelevant to the business at hand.

Out of Order

Someone is not following *Robert's Rules of Order* and is speaking out of turn.

Table a Motion

Additional information is required before a decision can be made; the item in question is deferred to the next meeting.

Adjournment

This represents a formal end to the meeting.

HIGHLIGHTING AND ANNOTATING CORRESPONDENCE

Highlighting

- Use a highlighter or underline using pencil (yellow highlighter is best for photocopying because it does not show).
- Highlight sparingly.
- Look for key words.
- Look for dates and times and the accuracy of them – check the calendar.
- Look for a reference to something that is being mailed separately (under separate cover).
- Look for items that request action to be taken.
- Scan tables of contents in magazines for relevant articles.
- Look for items to be entered as tasks or appointments in your calendar software.

Annotating

- Write in pencil in the margin or on the back of paper.
- Some bosses prefer that you not annotate or at least annotate in pencil so that the notations can be erased, because some correspondence must be forwarded to someone or circulated.
- Make brief notes.
- Include reminders that you would give your boss if you were speaking with him or her.
- If something requested has been done, write "done" or "received" in the margin – e.g., mailing or receiving of an item under separate cover.
- Notes such as "You are available," "Are you attending?" and "I will confirm for you" are examples of written conversation between you and your boss.
- Some may prefer that you annotate on the back.
- If money is attached, make sure that the cheque matches the amount owed.
- Check amounts on invoices for accuracy.

JOIN.ME FOR ONLINE COLLABORATION (Page 1)

1. **To create a Join.me account:**

   a. Start Internet Explorer and key **join.me** in the address bar.

   b. Click on the **Free Trial** button at the top right of the window.

   c. Under **Sign Up**, type your school email address and password in the appropriate fields; click **Create Account** (you may want to deselect **Keep me logged**).

   d. Under **Start Meeting**, select the arrow. Join.me software will be downloaded to your computer and a dialogue box will appear in which a link will be displayed.

2. **To initiate a meeting:**

   a. Click the link; a drop-down menu appears in which you can choose to copy the link to the clipboard.

   b. Paste the link into an email that you will now send meeting participants.

3. **To join a meeting:**

   a. In your Inbox, open the email sent to you by the person initiating the meeting; copy the join.me link.

   b. Start Internet Explorer and paste the join.me link into the address bar.

   c. A dialog box may appear indicating that a locked meeting is in progress; key your name and click **knock to join**.

4. **To accept someone asking to join a meeting:**

   a. When someone clicks knock to join, a dialog box will appear asking whether you would like the participant to join; click **Yes**.

JOIN.ME FOR ONLINE COLLABORATION (Page 2)

5. **To view the list of participants:**

   a. In the **join.me** toolbar, click the **Participant** icon (second from last) to see the list of participants.

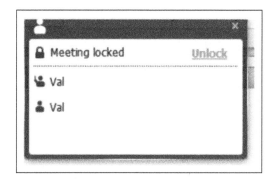

   b. Click the **Unlock** button if you would like others to join without clicking the **knock to join** button (note that they would still need the join.me link from you to join); the option is available to the chair.

6. **To chat:**

   a. Click the **Chat** icon and begin a discussion with those participating in the meeting.

7. **To give a presentation:**

   a. Open the presentation.

   b. Move through each of the slides; the participants should be able to view the presentation (maximize the window if necessary).

8. **To request control of the screen:**

   a. Use **Chat** to ask for control.

9. **To give control of the screen:**

   a. Click the **Share control** button in the join.me toolbar and click the participant's name.

JOIN.ME FOR ONLINE COLLABORATION (Page 3)

10. **To stop sharing:**

    a. Click the **Stop sharing control** button.

11. **To send the participant a file:**

    a. Click the **Participants** button and move to the icon representing the participant.

    b. Action icons will appear to the left of the name of the person; click the **Send file** icon.

    c. An Open dialog box will appear; navigate to the folder in which the file you wish to send is located and double-click to send the file.

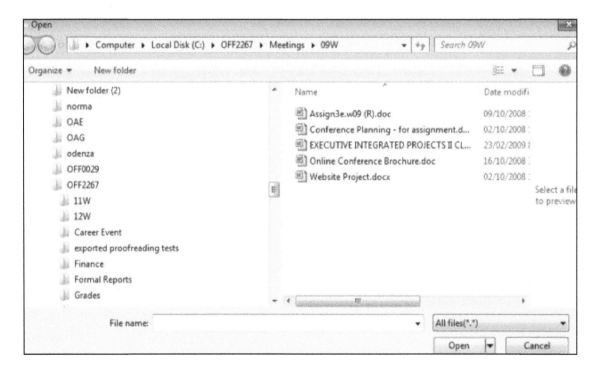

JOIN.ME FOR ONLINE COLLABORATION (Page 4)

12. **To accept a sent file:**

    a. A dialog box should appear once the file has been sent to you; click **Yes** to accept it.

    b. A Save As dialog box will appear; select a folder to which you would like the file to be saved and click **Save**.

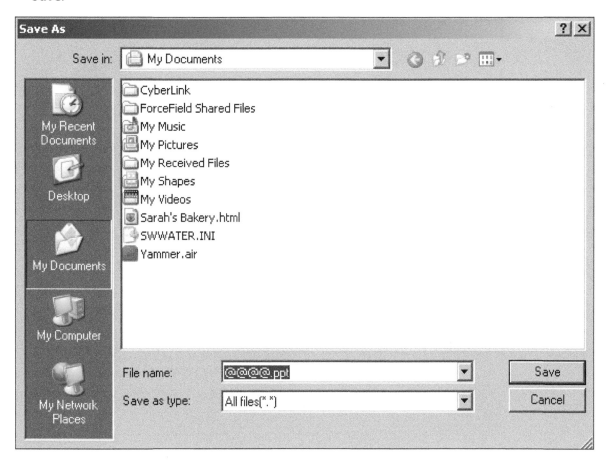

JOIN.ME FOR ONLINE COLLABORATION (Page 5)

13.   **To leave the meeting:**

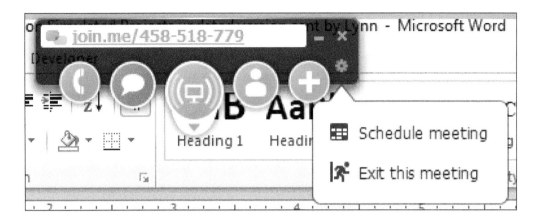

a. Click the orange wheel below the orange x on the right side of the join.me window.

b. Click **Exit this meeting**.

LABELS

- Use MS Word.
- Go to **Mailings**.
- Go to **Labels**.
- Select **Single Label**.
- Insert Row No. and Column No.
- Go to **Options**.
- Go to **Printer Information**.
- Tray: Select **Manual**.
- Under label vendors, select **Avery US Letter**.
- Select **5159**.

MEETINGS – AN INTRODUCTION

Meetings are intended to provide information and a forum in which decisions can be made. The administrative assistant may be responsible for performing the following tasks:

- Checking the availability of key participants

- Arranging date and time

- Reserving a suitable meeting room

- Sending the meeting notice

- Preparing, finalizing, and distributing the agenda

- Ensuring that appropriate supplies and equipment are available and in working condition (e.g., name tags, whiteboard markers, chairs, audiovisual and telecommunications devices, etc.)

- Ordering refreshments including food if the meeting is long; consideration should be given for those with dietary restrictions

- Preparing, assembling, and distributing other materials if required, such as documents related to agenda items; these should be distributed before the meeting so that participants can review their contents

- Ensuring that copies of the previous meeting minutes and agenda are available

- Preparing seating arrangements

- Attending the meeting

- Handling the telephone and other interruptions

- Recording meeting discussions and decisions

- Ensuring that the meeting room is returned to its original state (e.g., return equipment, collect extra copies of documents)

- Preparing, editing, and distributing the meeting's minutes

MINUTES OF MEETINGS (Page 1)

Minutes are the official record of what has occurred during a meeting. The minutes represent topics discussed, decisions made, and tasks assigned.

Taking minutes is an important task because the minutes are considered legal evidence of what happened in the meeting.

Purpose

- Provides an objective summary of the proceedings
- Updates those who are unable to attend
- Represents a reminder of action to be taken
- Serves as a rationale for the decisions made
- Serves as a legal document; if approved, they can be used in legal proceedings

Role of the Minute Taker

- Takes attendance at the meeting
- Produces an accurate summary of the meeting within a reasonable time period
- Ensures that the chair validates the minutes by signing the minutes
- Stores the minutes and all related materials

Steps to Ensure Effective Minute Taking

- Determine the purpose of the meeting.
- Review the last meeting minutes to better understand what is being discussed.
- While taking minutes, put notations in the text wherever the information requires clarification.
- Arrange in advance with the chair a signal to be used if help is required during the meeting.

Methods to Record Minutes

A. Voice Recorder

- Useful in preparing a verbatim transcript (may be necessary in a formal meeting)
- Requires the permission of everyone
- Should also take minutes either by hand or using a laptop in case the recorder fails or the sound is not clear, and to record important details that cannot be captured by the recorder such as a nod of the head indicating agreement

B. Shorthand

- Take shorthand using a steno pad because the vertical line down the middle encourages the use of bullets and keywords.

MINUTES OF MEETINGS (Page 2)

C. Laptop

- Efficient because first draft already keyed
- Allows access to resources such as the Internet and email during meeting

Preparing Minutes

Immediately following the meeting, the notes will need to be converted into a set of minutes. This should be done as soon as possible while memory is fresh. The following represents some of the steps an administrative assistant may undertake:

- Review previously prepared minutes when preparing them for the first time to ensure consistent format and content.
- Prepare a draft of the minutes double spaced and have the chair review this draft.
- Distribute the minutes to the other participants once they are approved by the chair.
- Once the minutes have been distributed, wait for requests for amendments.
- When minutes have been amended, record the changes.

Format of the Minutes

The format should be established before minutes are taken at a meeting.

- Formal meetings follow *Robert's Rules of Order* to ensure order and legality.
- Most meetings use a less formal set of procedures or rules sometimes referred to as "Bob's Rules of Order."

What Minutes Should Include

- Attachments from the agenda (may not be distributed to everyone; but should be included with the file copy)
- The word "minutes" at the top of the document
- The title of meeting (this could include name of company or organization)
- The date and time (on which meeting was held, not when the minutes were prepared)
- The location
- Attendance:
  - A list of names of those who attended the meeting and those who were invited but did not attend should be included
  - A list of those who notified the administrative assistant of their absence in advance (absent with regrets) and those who did not (absent)
  - A list of those who are not regular members as "Guests"
  - Identification of the chair and minute taker

MINUTES OF MEETINGS (Page 3)

- Arrangement of the names alphabetically by last name or in rank order; consistency should be applied when listing names (e.g., full first and last name)

- A record of the time of a member's late arrival or early departure as attendance can be used to show quorum

The remaining items will likely be included in a set of **formal** meeting minutes but not in informal meeting minutes:

- Call to order

- Approval of agenda

- Approval, amendment, or correction of the last meeting minutes

- Unfinished business from the last meeting minutes

- Reports

- Finances

- Correspondence

- New business: include motions, concerns, and questions raised

- For decisions made, the rationale of the decision

- The date and time of the next meeting (may not be decided at meeting; can include at bottom of minutes once determined)

- Adjournment

- The signature of the chair and secretary and the date of approval (when minutes are to be distributed)

What Minutes Should Not Include

- Social exchanges

- Personal and minor details

- Verbatim conversations

- Opinions

- Anything that happened **after** the meeting

NOTICES OF MEETINGS

The meeting notice is used to inform participants of an upcoming meeting's details (subject, date, location). Notices are sent by email, email attachment, or by letter mail.

The meeting should be announced as soon as possible. Participants will need to review materials, conduct research, and create documents, so that they will be fully prepared for the meeting. Notification of formal meetings and conferences could be made as early as three or more months in advance. By-laws of the group must be respected because they may affect content and/or timing of notice.
Details of the notice include:

- The name or purpose of the meeting

- Time

- Date

- Location

- A request for agenda items, with an estimate of the time required to discuss the topic and an indication of any special requirements for equipment such as a laptop

- A request to confirm attendance by a specified date

NOTICES OF MEETINGS USING EVITE (Page 1)

Particularly for formal meetings, participants may not work within the same organization. As a result, an online tool such as Evite is useful to ensure that the notice for the meeting is delivered to everyone. To use Evite, go to the following site:

http://www.evite.com

Create an Account

1. Click on **Register** and complete the form. Use your email account information.

2. Check your Inbox; you will be asked to confirm your registration.

3. A dialog box will appear that includes a verification code. Click **Submit** in the dialog box.

4. A **Verify Account** dialog box will appear indicating that your account was successfully verified. Click **Close**.

Create a Notice of Meeting in Evite

1. At the top of the Evite window, click **Create an Invitation**.

2. At the top of the window, select a design category for your invitation.

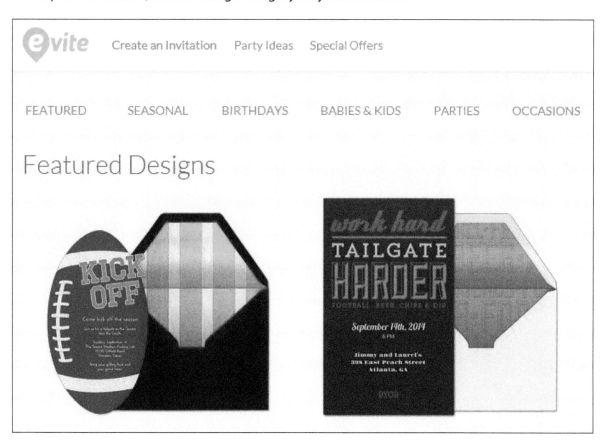

NOTICES OF MEETINGS USING EVITE (Page 2)

3. Use the scroll button to view the available designs within your selected category.

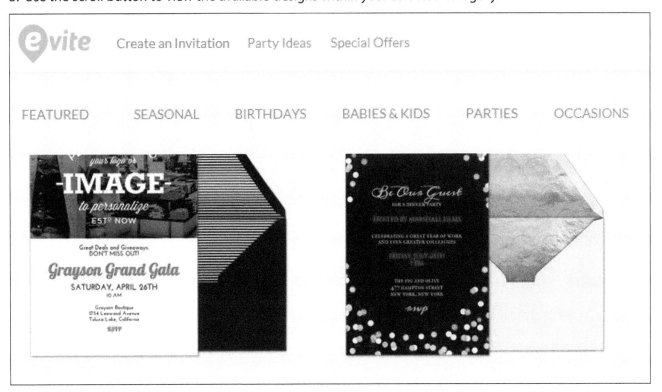

4. Click to select the desired design. The **Enter Details** window now appears.

5. Complete the required details (e.g., Event Title, Type, Host name, etc.).

NOTICES OF MEETINGS USING EVITE (Page 3)

6. In the message field, compose a message appropriate for a notice of meeting:

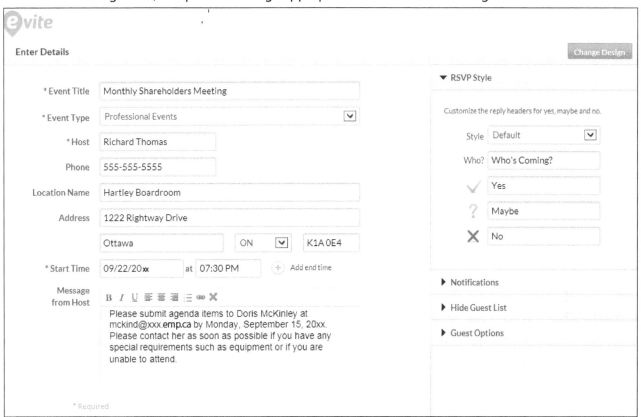

7. Select the desired options under RSVP Style.

8. Click **Cancel** if you wish to cancel your selections and start again. Click **Save Draft** if you would like to save your selections and continue editing during another session. Click **Preview Invitation** to view the notice; click the **Close** button at the top of the preview window to return to the **Enter Details** window.

9. Click **Continue** to move the next step.

10. In the **Add Guests** window, key the email addresses of those you wish to invite. Note that you are instructed to separate each address by a comma or a hard return. Once you have added each person's email address, click **Add Guest**. Note that you may go **Back to Enter Details** (the previous step), **Save Draft** (to resume at a later time), or **Preview Invitation** by clicking the appropriate buttons at the bottom of the window.

11. Once all the guests have been added, click **Finish and Send**. After a few moments, you will view a *Captcha* dialog box that will instruct you to key a set of characters. Once you have completed this step, click on **Submit**. A message confirming the delivery of your notice will then appear.

12. To log out of Evite, click the down arrow to the right of your name in the upper right corner of the Evite window. Click **Sign Out**.

NOTICES OF MEETINGS USING EVITE (Page 4)

Respond to a Notice of Meeting in Evite

1. To respond to a notice from Evite, go to your Inbox and open the email from Evite.

2. Click on the title link or **View this Invitation** to open the invitation. The complete invitation will appear.

3. Below the notice window, select your response to the invitation. A comment box will become available in which a message can be keyed (e.g., in the event that you have an agenda item to submit). Click **Reply**.

View the Responses to a Notice in Evite

1. To view the guest list and any comments that may have been submitted, log in to Evite.

2. Under **Upcoming Events**, click the title of your event. Evite will keep track of the number of individuals who have responded and display these on the window's left side. Comments submitted will appear under **Event Conversation**.

3. To log out of Evite, click the down arrow to the right of your name in the upper right corner of the Evite window. Click **Sign Out**.

PERSONAL SKILLS INVENTORY

Divide a page into two columns. In the first column, make a list of any paid or volunteer work activities you have been involved in. In the second column, list the skills you have gained from your involvement in all of these paid and/or volunteer situations.

For example:
Fundraising Campaign Officer
Canadian Cancer Society
Daffodil Campaign

- *Interpersonal Communications*
- *Leadership*
- *Conflict Resolution*
- *Time Management*
- *Conceptual*
- *Technical Communication*
- *Organizational*
- *Setting Up Meetings*
- *Travel Arrangements*
- *Creating Reports*
- *Bookkeeping*

Note: These skills are only a few of the many other skills you may identify. All are transferable into any position you will have in the future. Do not underestimate any skills you identify. You *may not* use all of these skills in every résumé but you will have the list to pick and choose from as you apply for jobs throughout the years ahead.

PORTFOLIO

A portfolio is a binder or folder that contains, in an organized and methodical fashion, all of your prized work that you wish to showcase. Examples of items that you may want to put in your portfolio:

- Your best work (samples of computer-created documents)
- Certificates of achievement (related to the position sought)
- A copy of your résumé
- Reference letters

Organizing a portfolio helps you to recall all that you have done and prepare you for an interview. In addition, it helps you in responding to questions during the interview. You can quickly find a document in your portfolio to demonstrate a skill you may be discussing.

When you arrive at an interview with a portfolio under your arm, it demonstrates to the interviewer that you have gone an extra step to emphasize your desire to work for this organization. Many résumés and interviews are fairly standard. It can be difficult for an interviewer to decide who would be the best fit. A portfolio may be the deciding factor.

Creating a portfolio with quality paper, a table of contents, and an organized flow to the documents demonstrates the following skills:

- Time management
- Organizational
- Accuracy
- Knowledge-based

REPORTS

Format

- Centre information on the title page (vertically and horizontally).
- Change the top margin to 2 inches on the table of contents.
- Change the top margin to 2 inches on Page 1 of the report.
- Ensure that a 1-inch top margin is used on subsequent pages.
- Use 1-inch side margins.
- Use a 1-inch bottom margin.
- Double space before and after tables.
- Use side headings; bold and use either all caps or title case with underlining.
- Paginate all pages at bottom and right.

Steps for Creating Title Page, Table of Contents, and Breaks

- In a blank document, ensure that your name is at the top of the report, and create a Next Page section break.
- Do not use the Cover Page option. It may cause you difficulties when inserting your page numbering.
- Create your cover page making sure to include all appropriate information. Make sure your insertion point is at the end of the text on the cover page.
- Go to Page Layout. Insert a Next Page section break. Save. Insert another Next Page section break before the body of your report.
- Go to View. Choose Draft and make sure your document is properly subdivided into sections. You should see Section 1 (cover page), Section 2 (table of contents), and Section 3 (body of the report). If correct, save at this point. If not, correct your errors.
- Go back to print layout view. Appropriately select the text for the table of contents.
- Go to the page designated for the table of contents. Generate it. Save.
- Make sure your insertion point is at the bottom of the page containing the Table of Contents. It should not be in the box containing the Table of Contents.
- Go to Insert. Select Page Number. Choose Bottom of Page and align at the right.
- Select Page Number. Select Format Page Numbers. In the "Number Format" drop-down list, choose the Roman numeral option (i, ii, iii). Make sure the link to previous is not selected and that no page number appears on the cover page. If a page number does appear on the first page, simply delete it.
- Go to the top of the page containing the first page of the report.
- Go to page numbering. Change the formatting to Arabic numbers (1, 2, 3).

REQUEST FOR PROPOSAL (RFP)

This is a form that an organization uses to elicit bids from potential vendors for a product or service. The purpose is to have several companies bid on the work, thus producing the best price.

The organization can take steps to minimize errors and ensure that bids match what it really needs. The RFP should provide its requirements in detail. Specific dates should be indicated including the due date for submission and date on which the decision will be made. It should also be made available to prospective vendors as early as possible.

REQUEST FOR PROPOSAL TEMPLATE WITH EXPLANATION (Page 1)

Berry, Duthie & Miller

REQUEST FOR PROPOSAL

Submission Requirements   (to be completed by you)

Submission Due Date		Time
Submission Method		

Contact Information   (to be completed by you)

General	
Company/Organization Name	
Address 1	
Address 2	
City	Province
Postal Code	
Contact Person	
Salutation	
Last Name	First Name
Phone	Fax
Email Address	

Facility Information   (to be completed by you)

General	
Name	
Address	
City	Province
Postal Code	Phone
Fax Number	Email
Web Address	

REQUEST FOR PROPOSAL TEMPLATE WITH EXPLANATION (Page 2)

General Meeting Requirements   **(to be completed by you)**

Meeting Name	
Dates	
Function Start Date	Function End Date
Arrival Date	Departure Date
Number of People	
Notes	

Meeting Room(s)   **(highlighted areas to be completed by you)**

General	
Start Date	End Date
Capacity	Setup Type
Equipment and Furniture	

☐ Chairs	☐ Tables	☐ Microphone
☐ Projector	☐ Videotaping	☐ Wireless Internet Access
☐ Screen	☐ Video Projector	

Other (Specify)
Services

☐ Setup	☐ Cleanup	☐ Other

Accommodations   **(highlighted areas to be completed by you)**

Check-in Time	Check-out Time
Single Number Required	Cost per night
Double Number Required	Cost per night
Suite Number Required	Cost per night

REQUEST FOR PROPOSAL TEMPLATE WITH EXPLANATION (Page 3)

Amenities

☐ Business Services	☐ Fitness Centre	☐ Golf
☐ High Speed Internet	☐ Indoor Pool	☐ Outdoor Pool
☐ Parking		
Other		

Food and Beverage

(select each meal in Required checkbox and indicate date(s) meal is required under Description/Notes)

Type	Required	Cost of each	Description/Notes (i.e., if event is +1 day, indicate dates required)
Breakfast	☐	$	
Lunch	☐	$	
Reception	☐	$	
Dinner	☐	$	
Breaks	☐	$	

RESEARCHING POTENTIAL EMPLOYERS

There are many ways to conduct research on a potential employer. The list includes websites, blogs, discussion boards, Facebook, Twitter, online business magazines, newspapers, and television or radio.

Company Websites, Blogs, Twitter, and Facebook

Company website/blog/Twitter/Facebook sites provide a voice for a company that educates and informs website visitors. These organizational social media options showcase what the organization is all about: What do they sell? What do they purchase? What do they make? What is it like to work there? What is their annual profit/loss? Who are their competitors? Who are their clients? Who are their customers? How many locations does the company have? Are they national/international? Where is the head office? Who is in charge? How many employees does the company have? How long has the organization been established? Does the company give back to the community around it?

Professional Associations

If you belong to a professional association, attend a meeting or check the website to see what networking opportunities are available. If you do not, consider joining an association in the administrative field. Word-of-mouth (networking) is an important way of finding out about opportunities.

Read Anything You Can

If you are interested in finding a position locally, the business section of your local newspaper is a great way to keep up to date. The business section will have articles on new companies and changes in established businesses.

Most magazines and newspapers have articles that you can read online. An organization moving into your city might create an opportunity for employment. Never underestimate any news you may hear.

It is never a waste of time to constantly be researching anything on the topic of business. Tell everyone you know that you are looking for work. Every conversation, whether personal or professional, can represent a networking opportunity.

RÉSUMÉ WRITING

Résumés – Chronological/Functional

A chronological résumé is a summary of all you have done (paid or volunteer employment) described in reverse chronological order (i.e., beginning with your most **recent** experiences). Candidates who have worked many years in an industry without any gaps prefer chronological résumés. This style of résumé shows candidates' loyalty to one organization, or more, in the years they have dedicated, as well as a consistent upgrading in training and experience in their field.

A functional résumé is a highlight of what you have done (paid or volunteer employment). This list does not have to be in chronological order. Instead, the focus is on identifying your most important skills and from which organization you have acquired them. Candidates who have worked with many different organizations or have had gaps in their experience prefer to use functional résumés.

Skills

You may have many transferable skills from different positions (both paid and volunteer) and may like to describe them in a comprehensive list. Candidates who have not had a lot of experience find that a skills category helps them to showcase their strengths. Use the work and volunteer experience areas to further explain those skills.

Format

A résumé should be no longer than two pages. The second page should have a header on it to indicate your name and the page number.

A reader should find a lot of white space on any résumé. If the page looks too crowded, the reader will lose interest or become overwhelmed.

Objective

The objective of a résumé is to obtain an interview. Know what you are saying and how you are saying it! Be honest! Your résumé will be referred to in any interview and you must be able to demonstrate you have the skills indicated in it.

Also remember that a résumé is a summary. Avoid writing lengthy sentences with too much information; use bullets instead.

SCHEDULING MEETINGS USING MS OUTLOOK (Page 1)

Viewing Another Person's Calendar

To view another person's Calendar in order to determine their availability for a meeting:

1. Click the down arrow beside **Share** in the toolbar.

2. Click **Open a Shared Calendar**.

3. Click **Name**.

4. Select by double-clicking the name of the person whose Calendar you wish to view and click **OK**.

5. A dialog box will display confirming your desire to open the shared Calendar; click on **OK** to confirm. Under Calendars in the Navigation pane, the name of the person whose Calendar you added will appear under **People's Calendars**. That person's Calendar will now appear alongside yours.

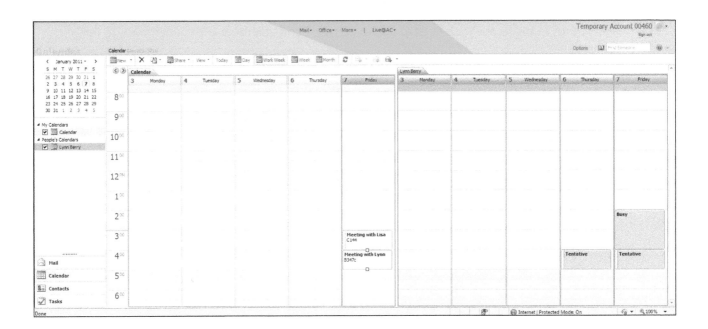

SCHEDULING MEETINGS USING MS OUTLOOK (Page 2)

To view a person's Calendar in a separate window:

1. Right-click the person's name in the Navigation pane.

2. In the shortcut menu that displays, select **Open in a New Window**.

To turn off the display of another person's Calendar:

1. Click the check box to the left of the person's name in the Navigation pane (note: if you can't see the person's name, click the People's Calendar link to expand the list).

To remove another person's Calendar:

1. Right-click the person's name in the Navigation pane.

2. Click **Remove Shared Calendar**.

Share a Calendar

You can invite anyone in your shared Address Book to share your Calendar. By doing so, you can control the amount of detail they can view.

1. In Calendar, click **Share** in the toolbar.

2. Click **Share a Calendar**; a **Sharing Invitation** dialog box will be displayed.

3. Click **To:** the Address Book dialog box will be displayed.

4. Key the person's name to locate the person in your system. Select by double-clicking the name of the person with whom you wish to share your Calendar and click **OK**.

5. In the **Sharing Invitation** dialog box, select the amount of detail you wish this person to view:
   - **Free/busy information** to share only free/busy information.
   - **Free/busy information including subject and location** to add the subject and location to what the invitee can view.
   - **All information** to let the invitee to see your free/busy information, subject, location, and other message details.

6. Click **I want to request permission to view the recipient's Calendar folder** to automatically request permission to view the recipient's Calendar.

7. Key a message, if desired. Click **Send**. The request will appear as a message in the recipient's Inbox.

8. To accept an invitation to share a Calendar, click **Add This Calendar** in the toolbar.

9. To share a Calendar when you receive an invitation, click **Share My Calendar**.

SCHEDULING MEETINGS USING MS OUTLOOK (Page 3)

Deleting a Shared Permission in a Calendar

You can easily restore a Calendar once it has been removed. Further, you will continue to view its details. To ensure that the details have been removed, you'll need to delete the Calendar's shared permissions.

To delete shared permissions:

1. In **Calendar**, click **Share**.

2. Click **Change Sharing Permissions – Calendar**.

3. In the dialog box that displays, click the name of the person with whom you no longer wish to share your Calendar.

4. Click the **Delete** button in the toolbar.

5. Click **Yes** to confirm that you wish to delete permission to share the Calendar.

Scheduling a Meeting

You can use Outlook to schedule a meeting and/or resources such as rooms. Use the Calendar to send meeting requests and reserve resources. Responses to your meetings appear in your Inbox.

To schedule a meeting:

1. Click the down arrow beside **New**.

2. Select **Meeting Request**.

3. In the **To** and **Optional** text boxes, enter the names of the people whom you want to receive this meeting request. You can specify a conference room or special equipment, such as an overhead projector, in the **Resources** box.

4. In the **Start time** and **End time** lists, select the appropriate dates and times. If you want the meeting to occur regularly, click **Repeat** ↻.

5. In the **Show time as** list, select how you want your schedule to appear for the duration of the meeting. Your selection (**Busy**, **Free**, **Tentative**, or **Away**) is what other people see when they view your schedule and the schedules of all attendees.

6. Select the **Reminder** check box to be reminded about this meeting. This also reminds all recipients of the meeting request if they have reminders enabled on their Calendars.

7. Type a message to accompany your meeting request in the message text area, and then click ▦ **Send**. A meeting request is sent to each attendee, and the new meeting is added to your schedule. Each person who receives your meeting request can accept, decline, or accept it tentatively.

SCHEDULING MEETINGS USING MS OUTLOOK (Page 4)

Scheduling Assistant

Alternatively, you can take advantage of the Scheduling Assistant in Calendar to help you find the best time to schedule a meeting. The Scheduling Assistant compares the calendars of attendees and resources to help you find a time when everyone is available.

To use the Scheduling Assistant:

1. Create a new appointment or meeting request, and then click the **Scheduling Assistant** tab.

2. Click **Select Attendees** to open the **Address Book** window and select those you wish to invite. The availability chart automatically displays all your attendees' schedules on the day of your meeting with the time of your meeting highlighted. A blue bar in the schedule window next to a name means that person is busy at that time.

3. To change the meeting date, click the **Start** or **End** box, and then select a new meeting date.

4. To move the meeting time, click the centre of the highlighted bar that represents the meeting time, and then drag the meeting to a different time.

5. After you verify availability, click the **Appointment** tab to finish filling out your meeting request.

Next to the availability chart is a summary of attendee availability. The summary offers a list of possible meeting times in addition to how many selected attendees and resources are available at each time.

To see the details of a specific time, click the time in the **Suggested Times** list. To see possible times on other days, click the calendar in the **Suggested Times** pane. Clicking a time in the **Suggested Times** list automatically changes the meeting to that time.

You can use the **Scheduling Assistant** toolbar to change the date, start time, and end time of the meeting. You can use the **Suggested Times** window to change the date and duration of your meeting and to select a suggested time.

The **Scheduling Assistant** has an option on its toolbar to show only working hours. If this is selected and one or more attendees don't have working hours that overlap with the other attendees, the **Scheduling Assistant** will show that it couldn't find any available times for the meeting. This frequently happens for meetings that include attendees in multiple time zones. You can turn off **Show only working hours** to see possible meeting times.

Modifying a Meeting

You can change the details of a meeting you had previously scheduled.

To change a meeting:

1. In Calendar, double-click the meeting you wish to change.

2. In the meeting request form, make the necessary changes (e.g., add new attendees, change the location, start and end times, etc.).

3. On the toolbar, select **Send Update**.

SCHEDULING MEETINGS USING MS OUTLOOK (Page 5)

Cancelling a Meeting

You can cancel a meeting by simply deleting it from your Calendar. Note that you cannot cancel a meeting you did not create. You can only remove the meeting from your own Calendar. When you do, you'll be given the option of sending a response to the meeting organizer. If you do not, the meeting organizer will not know that you are not attending the meeting.

To cancel a meeting:

1. In Calendar, select the meeting you wish to cancel.

2. Click the **Delete** ✗ button in the toolbar.

3. Click ▤ **Send** to send a cancellation notice to attendees.

Replying to a Meeting Request

Other people may invite you to a meeting. These invitations appear in your Inbox as meeting requests. You have several options for replying.

To reply to a meeting request:

1. In your Inbox, select the meeting request.

2. Click on one of the options to reply:

   ✓ **Accept** – Accepts the meeting and adds it to your Calendar. Other people looking at your Calendar will see that you are busy during the scheduled time.

   ❓ **Tentative** – Accepts the meeting but indicates that you may not attend it. The meeting is also added to your Calendar. Other people looking at your Calendar will see that you are tentatively scheduled for the meeting time.

   ✗ **Declines** – Declines the meeting. Nothing is added to your Calendar. This also deletes the meeting request from your Inbox.

3. Clicking on either of the above options opens a menu that includes: **Edit the response before sending**, **Send the response now**, or **Don't send a response**. Select the desired option. If you select **Edit the response before sending**, a message window that's addressed to the sender of the meeting request opens. To add more recipients to your meeting response, type their names on the To and Cc lines. Type a message in the text box. For example, you can explain why you may not attend the meeting.

4. When you're finished writing your response, click ▤ **Send**.

Note: If you have a conflict in your Calendar, you will see a banner in the heading of the meeting request. Click the banner to view the details of the conflict.

SURVEY – PAPER FORMAT (Page 1)

Who: Stakeholders, focus groups, and participants

What: Questionnaire

When: Immediately after the event or during the event (fresh in minds)

How: Select best method: email, mail, telephone, in person, online

Why: Feedback to make changes, provide validation, or determine needs

Design of Survey

- Determine the purpose – make sure you understand it.

- Follow the KISS principle (keep it simple).

- Ask only *need to know* questions where you will be able to use the information upon collection and analysis.

- Remain objective.

- Prepare only one page if possible (legal size if need be).

- Include a title.

- Start with a preamble (indicate the purpose of the survey).

- Design a series of questions that will provide the data to meet your purpose.

- Be careful to choose the right words so that you don't cause confusion or lack of interpretation.

- Use parallelism; ensure that the same verb tense is being used and if you are using "ing" endings, be consistent.

- Allow *not applicable* or *don't know* responses to all questions.

- Include *other* or *none* responses if possible depending upon the question.

- If asking sensitive questions such as salary or age, provide ranges to the answers.

- Have text to the right of the answer box.

- Questions are to be numbered.

- Only have one question per number.

- Keep some flow of thought through the survey; use a logical sequence and ensure that the language is non-threatening.

- Include a thank you.

- You may want to provide space for respondents to provide other comments at the bottom of the survey.

- Include logos if available.

- Be aware of white space, alignment, and ease of reading and understanding questions.

- Ensure that the survey is dated at the bottom.

SURVEY – PAPER FORMAT (Page 2)

Types of Questions

- Multiple choice
- Open-ended; numeric or text; opinions are expressed
- Closed questions (yes/no responses)

Types of Rating Scales

- Excellent, good, fair, poor
- 1 to 10
- 1 to 5
- Strongly agree, agree, disagree, strongly disagree, neither agree nor disagree
- Yes, no, maybe

Negative Questions

- Keep questions positive.
- When a question is answered in the negative, ask the respondent to explain the reason for the negative answer.

SURVEYMONKEY

1. Go to the SurveyMonkey website: http://www.surveymonkey.com.

2. Create an account by clicking the **Sign Up Free** button at the right side of the SurveyMonkey homepage.

3. Complete the account information. Take a screen shot of the account information and save it for future reference.

4. Click **Sign Up**.

5. At the top right corner of the SurveyMonkey screen, click **Create Survey**.

6. Under **Create a new survey**, key an appropriate title for your survey.

7. Under **Category**, select **Events**; click **Continue** at the lower right of the SurveyMonkey window.

8. If desired, select a theme under **Edit Survey**. This will change the colour of the header in your survey.

9. Under Page 1, select **Add a Question**. Key the text for your question.

10. Under **Question Type**, click the down arrow and select the type of question desired; you may be asked to select certain options based on the type of question selected, such as the display format and possible answers.

11. At the bottom of the window, select **Save & Add Next Question**.

12. Repeat steps 10 and 11 until you have all the desired questions.

13. Once you have completed the last question, click on **Save & Close**.

14. Review the questions you have prepared; click **Edit Question** to the right of the question number to change a question.

15. Review the appearance of the survey by clicking **Preview Survey** at the upper right of the window.

16. Once you are satisfied with the results, click **Send Survey** at the upper right of the window.

17. Under **Your Survey Web Link**, select and copy (Ctrl+c) the web link displayed.

18. Send those you wish to complete the survey an email that includes an appropriate subject line. In the body of the email, paste the web link.

TELECONFERENCING (Page 1)

Teleconferences are telecommunications-based meetings using different electronic equipment to make communication possible among three or more people at various locations. There are different types of meetings: audio conferences, video conferences, and web conferences.

Advantages of Teleconferences

Advantages of teleconferences include:

- Participants can be assembled on relatively short notice.
- Participants can be connected with each other at several unique locations.
- Travel time and expense are reduced.
- Administrative overhead associated with meetings is reduced.

1. Audio Conferences

During an audio conference, meeting participants at different locations are linked electronically by telephone. These online collaborations are relatively inexpensive and easy to set up. Audio conferences can be initiated by:

- A caller using a special "conference" feature on a business telephone set. The caller dials a number and asks the receiver of the call to hold while the caller repeats the process to add another person into the call.
- A local service provider or other communications company.

Follow these guidelines to ensure that the teleconference is effective:

- Use an agenda to keep the meeting on track.
- Identify yourself when speaking.
- Address participants by name when asking questions or making comments.
- Use a headset, if available; your hands will be free to take notes and perform other tasks.

2. Video Conferences

In video conferences, participants can see and hear one another using a combination of electronic equipment such as video or web cameras, computer monitors or projectors, microphones, and speakers. This method provides high quality teleconferences but setup can be challenging and expensive.

Follow these guidelines to ensure that the video conference is effective:

- Treat the camera as a participant by speaking directly to it.
- Minimize activities such as shuffling papers because they may be distracting to others.
- Prepare visual aids using large print sizes.
- Dress professionally.

TELECONFERENCING (Page 2)

3. Web Conferences

In web conferences, participants communicate using a computer, an Internet connection, and special software or go to special vendor-hosted websites such as **Join.me**. Web conferences are relatively inexpensive, easy to establish, and reliable.

Features can include:

- Whiteboard features for note taking
- Slide show features for running PowerPoint presentations
- The possibility of file downloads to the participants' computers to permit file sharing
- Options for audio and video communication.

TRANSCRIPTION (Page 1)

You will need the following equipment to install and use the transcription software referred to in this textbook:

- Computer
- Internet connection
- Headphones

The software to be used for the transcriptions in this textbook is called Express Scribe. Follow these steps to install the software:

1. Plug your headphones into the headphone jack on your computer or your computer's speakers.

2. Open your Internet browser and navigate to the following website:

   http://www.nch.com.au/scribe/index.html.

3. If this URL does not work, simply open your Internet browser, go to http://www.google.com and enter the words "express scribe free transcription software" into the search box. Then click on the resulting link to the new http://www.nch.emp.ca website.

4. Click the **Get it now** button.

5. Click **Run** on the following pop-up screen.

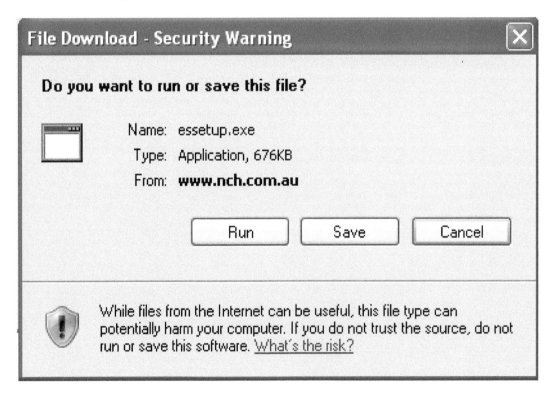

TRANSCRIPTION (Page 2)

6. Click **Run** again on the following pop-up screen.

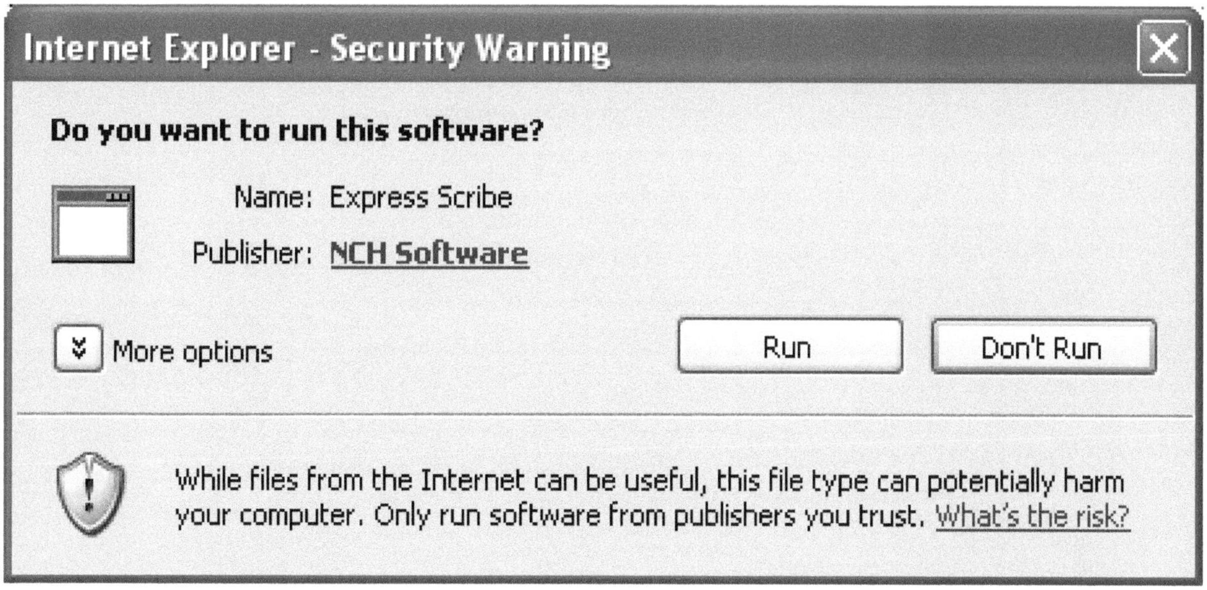

7. Click **Run** a third time on the following pop-up screen.

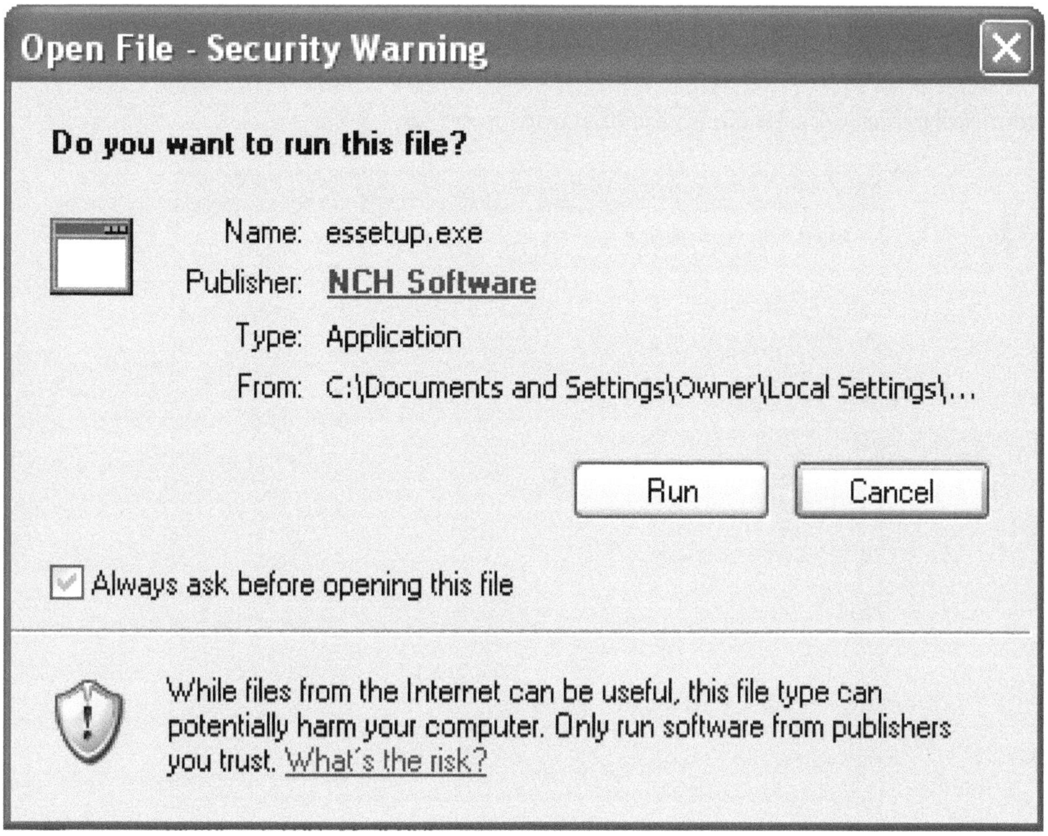

TRANSCRIPTION (Page 3)

8. The next screen will be the Express Scribe License Agreement. Click **I agree with these terms** and then click **Next**.

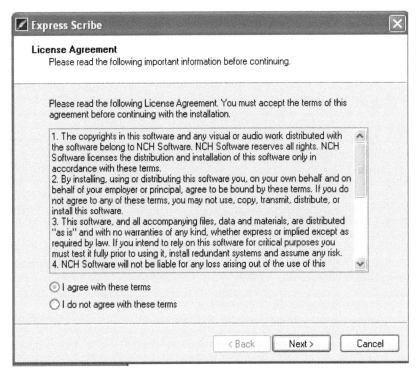

9. The program will install. Click **Finish** on the final pop-up screen.

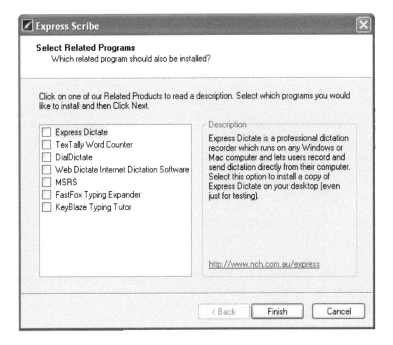

TRANSCRIPTION (Page 4)

10. The program will launch automatically, along with a recording of how to use the program.

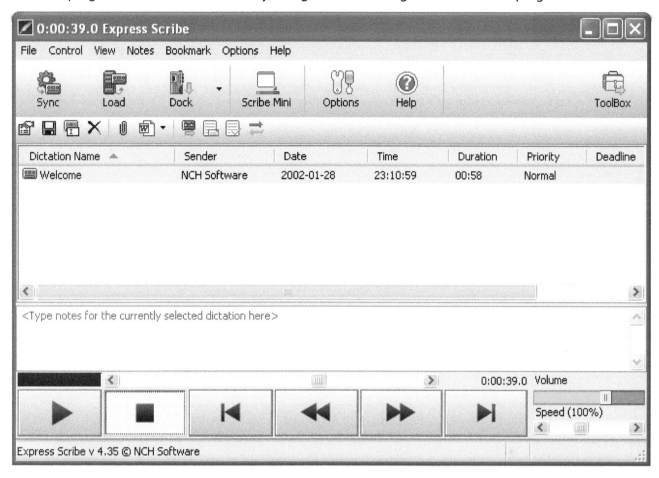

11. You can use the following hot keys to control the program:

1. F9 = Play
2. F4 = Stop
3. F7 = Rewind
4. F8 = Fast Forward
5. Ctrl+Home = Go to the beginning of the transcription
6. Ctrl+End = Go to the end of the transcription

Now that you have installed the required software, you need to create a folder on your computer's C:\ drive, or on a drive specified by your instructor, and call it "Transcription." Save all of your transcription files in this directory.

TRANSCRIPTION (Page 5)

To load voice files into the transcription software, click the **Load** button. Navigate to the newly created "Transcription" folder on your computer. Click **OK**, and you will see any voice files that are in your folder.

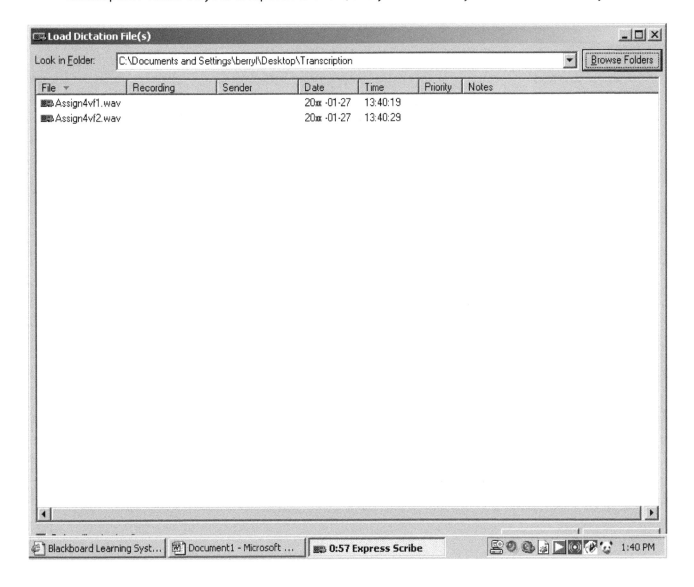

Click on a voice file to begin listening. Use the above keyboard shortcuts to stop and start as necessary. You may have your word processing software open for keying and minimize the Express Scribe software. You may use the keyboard shortcuts while the program is minimized.

TRAVEL AUTHORIZATION TEMPLATE WITH EXPLANATION (Page 1)

Berry, Duthie & Miller
Travel Authorization
General Information

Name: Blake Moore	Employee No.: 21244
Position: Director	Department: Marketing and Sales

Party to Visit: TSL Training Consultancy
Location: Berkshire, UK
Purpose of Trip: Product Demonstration

From: September 4, 20xx	To: September 8, 20xx

Estimated Cost

Account No.	Cost Centre	Location	Amount
3100-09	5300	UK	$4,400

Transportation

Air: ☒ Yes ☐ No	Rail: ☐ Yes ☒ No	Car: ☐ Yes ☒ No	Other:

Describe:
Ottawa–London–Ottawa

Accommodation

Required: ☒ Yes ☐ No	Number of Nights (inclusive): 4	From: September 4, 20xx	To: September 7, 20xx
Preferred:	(1) Hilton Inn	(2)	(3)

Travel Advance

Date Required: August 30, 20xx	Canadian	U.S.	Other
Cash (Max $150)	$ 70 **A**		40 GBP **B**
Company Cheque	$300 **C**		
Travellers' Cheques			
Total Advance	$370 **D**		
Foreign Exchange			1.81306 CAD **E**
Canadian Equivalent			$72.50 CAD **F**
Total Advance			$442.50 **G**

Authorization

Employee Signature: *Blake Moore*	Date: August 18, 20xx	Authorized By:	Date:

TRAVEL AUTHORIZATION TEMPLATE WITH EXPLANATION (Page 2)

Travel advance calculation:

1. Cell A: Estimate total required in Canadian cash (e.g., trip from office to airport; airport to home on return). In this example, it is estimated that a taxi from the office to the airport and from the airport to home will be around $35 per trip or $70 in total.

2. Cell B: Estimate total cash required in foreign funds (e.g., trip to and from the airport and the hotel). In this example, it is estimated that a trip from the airport to the hotel and from the hotel to the airport is around 40 GBP or 72.50 CAD.

3. Cell C: Estimate total cash expenses while in the foreign country (includes taxis, some meals, other incidentals; to do this, estimate a daily amount and multiply by the number of days). This will be deposited in the traveller's bank account for the traveller to draw from while away. In this example, it is estimated that total daily expenses while in London will be $100 per day or $300 in total (for a stay of 3 days; remember that most of the expenses are already covered on the travelling days).

4. **Cell D**: Subtotal the Canadian portion of the cash advance.

5. Cell E: Determine the rate to exchange foreign funds into Canadian funds.

6. Cell F: Convert the funds required in foreign currency in cell B into Canadian funds using the exchange rate in cell E (B × E).

7. **Cell G**: Calculate the total required in Canadian funds for the travel advance (A + C + F).

TRAVEL (INTERNATIONAL) ARRANGEMENTS (Page 1)

Many organizations have international interests that involve subsidiaries of the organization or relationships with other organizations. This may result in travel to foreign countries. The steps in planning a trip to a foreign country are similar to those used for domestic travel; for example, you may need to:

- Identify who is responsible for making arrangements (administrative assistant, other administrative assistant, in-house travel department, or travel agency).

- Know policies and procedures to be followed in making travel arrangements (class of travel to be used, type of ground travel permitted, air carrier preference, and per diem allowances).

The steps involved in arranging international travel include:

1. Planning the Trip

Gather information regarding the trip to make the travel arrangements. Details may include:

- The purpose of the trip
- The date of departure and return
- Companies the traveller plans to visit, including details such as telephone, fax, email, mailing addresses
- A list of documents, equipment, and other items that will be required, such as:
  - The travel authorization: This provides details of the trip and associated costs
  - The itinerary: This should include phone numbers (include instructions on how to place long distance and local calls within the country)
  - The travel advance: A small amount of cash should be provided to cover incidental expenses. The amount is included on the travel authorization. This cash should be provided in two currencies:
    - Domestic funds: A cash advance required to cover small expenses incurred before arrival in the destination country
    - Foreign funds: A small amount of cash in the currency of the destination country required for small expenses incurred when the traveller arrives
  - Company or personal credit card used to pay for other expenses
  - A passport; the document providing the traveller with permission to leave Canada and travel to other countries; applications and passport information on the Passport Canada website
  - A visa, if required; some countries require this special travel permit to be obtained prior to departure; check with the country's embassy
  - Electronic devices (e.g., a laptop, smartphone, etc.; note that voltage might not be the same in the foreign country)
  - International Driving Permit (IDP): likely required if the traveller plans to rent a car; obtained from the Canadian Automobile Association (CAA)
  - Travel insurance: medical and car insurance that may need to be purchased before leaving Canada; the company insurance plan may already cover the traveller

TRAVEL (INTERNATIONAL) ARRANGEMENTS (Page 2)

- Information regarding the destination, including:
  - Entry requirements such as passports and visas (see above)
  - Time zones: need to be considered when preparing itineraries and when placing calls to and from the destination country
  - Currency: the traveller will need to know where to get cash, such as the location of ATMs and banks if cash is required (a personal or company credit card is typically used to cover other expenses) and the rate at which this cash will be converted
  - Placing international phone calls (including codes and method such as cell phones, calling cards, and credit cards): for a cell phone, arrangements with the cell phone provider should be made prior to departure
  - Voltage for electrical devices: many devices will require an electrical charge. Possible requirements include a converter for non-continuous-use items such as hairdryers and transformers for continuous-use items such as laptops
  - Security issues: Is travel considered safe? What might the traveller do for protection? Check the Department of Foreign Affairs (DFAIT) website for the nearest location of consular assistance
  - Climate: influences what clothing to pack
  - Local laws and customs: the consequences if laws are violated or customs are not observed
  - Business etiquette: rules of conduct vary in different countries. Observance of the rules in the host country will ensure a more successful trip. For example, determine the importance of punctuality and the manner in which to address business counterparts
  - Health issues: conditions in the destination country may be quite different than in Canada. For example, tap water may not be safe to drink. Determine the health risks and learn preventive measures the traveller should take, including immunization requirements. The Centers for Disease Control (CDC), the World Health Organization (WHO), and the Public Health Agency of Canada provide general information regarding travel health. Travel health clinics can also provide advice on precautions to take
  - General information regarding the country such as its politics, economy, and culture. Knowledge is important; it demonstrates respect to the host and enables the visitor to engage in discussions that transcend business
- Air travel details including:
  - The preferred travel times, airline including loyalty program account number, and seat (aisle, inside, or window)
  - Baggage restrictions (check the airline and the Canadian Air Transport Security Authority for restrictions regarding weight, size, and contents of baggage)
  - Hotel preferences including the preferred location
- Meal preferences for meals on flights and at conferences; requests sometimes can be made in advance if the traveller has any dietary restrictions
- Ground transportation requirements, such as car rental, airport or hotel shuttle, or taxi

TRAVEL (INTERNATIONAL) ARRANGEMENTS (Page 3)

2. Making the Arrangements

Next, the actual arrangements based on the details collected during the planning phase will need to be made, including:

- Hotel reservations
- Airline reservations
- Reservations for ground transportation
- Preparing and assembling the material and equipment required (e.g., preparing the travel authorization and the itinerary and obtaining cash)

3. Performing Post-Trip Tasks

When the traveller returns, follow-up tasks may need to be performed, such as:

- Preparation of thank-you letters to the traveller's hosts
- Update of electronic documents
- Preparation of the travel expense claim

Appendix F

Related Task Documents

INVITATION LETTER   Project 1 – Task 1

CANADIAN SOCIETY FOR TRAINING

700 Spadina Avenue, Suite 300
Toronto, ON M5T 2T9

Tel: 416.467.5900 or 1.866.357.4275
Fax: 416.467.1642
http://www.ct.emp.ca
info@ct.emp.ca

September 4, 20xx

Mr. Grant Sagan
Director of Training
Berry, Duthie & Miller
820 - 360 Albert Street
Ottawa, ON K1R 7X7

Dear Mr. Sagan:

Re: National Conference in Vancouver, British Columbia

The annual conference this year is being held in Vancouver, British Columbia, from November 6 to 8, 20xx, inclusive, at the Westin Bayshore Hotel. We are beginning our quest for exciting guest speakers, and we have almost finished our journey should you agree to participate as one of our presenters. It would be a privilege if you would join us in our lineup.

The conference hours are 8 a.m. to 4 p.m. on November 6 and 7, and 8 a.m. to 1 p.m. on November 8 in the Baffin Room. We have reserved a 2 p.m. time slot on November 7 for you. This year's focus is Training in Our Economic Times. Since Berry, Duthie & Miller is a leader in this area, an overview of the current training situation in our nation's capital would be of value.

Would you be able to present at this year's session? We have allowed a time slot of approximately 15 minutes. This would be an excellent forum for marketing your organization.

Please confirm your attendance and your decision to be a presenter to me by September 28, 20xx. Should you be presenting, we require a short biography and passport-size photograph so we can include your information in our conference packages, which will be distributed by October 31, 20xx. Would you please email your biography, speech, and any associated PowerPoint presentation to Marie Beaudoin, our conference coordinator, at beaudoinm@ct.emp.ca by October 26, 20xx.

The registration fee is $2,500, and it is required with your acceptance of registration. Rooms have been reserved by the conference committee, and the charge is $125 per night for a single room, and $150 per night for a double room. We have arranged an exciting cruise on English Bay for the evening on November 7 commencing at 7 p.m. There is a small fee of $100 for this event, which needs to be enclosed separately with the registration fee.

We look forward to your participation and attendance at the conference.

Sincerely,

Anastasia Christian

Anastasia Christian
President

EMAIL FROM PRESIDENT   Project 1 – Task 18

To: sagan@bdm.emp.ca

Subject: Meeting in Victoria

Sorry, Grant, for the short notice. As you know, we have been working diligently at acquiring a training centre in Victoria. I had planned on flying out to a meeting scheduled for November 9, 20xx, with the Learning Academy, at their office with President Natasha Lightfoot from noon to 2 p.m., and I need you to attend on my behalf. Unfortunately, I have a conflict in my schedule.

Since you are in Vancouver already, I hope you can accommodate this request.

This is a luncheon meeting.

The following is the contact information:

Learning Academy
1123 Blanshard Street
Victoria, BC V8W 2H7

(250) 325-1232 [telephone]
(250) 325-0401 [fax]
www.learningacademy.com

Give me a call, and I will bring you up to speed.

Thanks.

Lynn

Lynn Berry
President
Berry, Duthie & Miller

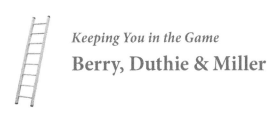

Keeping You in the Game
Berry, Duthie & Miller

INTEROFFICE MEMORANDUM

To: Administrative Assistant

From: Director of Marketing and Sales

Date: Today's Date

Subject: Marketing Fair

I would like to organize a marketing fair for the first Wednesday in February in the auditorium.

The purpose of this fair is for employers to showcase their companies to our graduates in the following areas:

- Finance
- Human Resources
- Software Applications
- Office Administration
- Business Administration

I would like one representative from each area to present, so I need you to assemble a database that includes two major companies in each of these areas. Next, prepare an invitation to *one* company in each area. Once the replies are received, we will determine whether we need to continue to fill the spots.

I was thinking that the event would occur from 1 to 4 p.m., and each presenter would be allotted 30 minutes. You will have to arrange for a coffee break of 15 minutes in the middle of the event, and I would like the presenters to attend a luncheon in our boardroom from 12 to 12:45 p.m.

I am also thinking that we need to advertise this event to our graduates; perhaps place a flyer on the bulletin boards and send an email to each graduate.

Please see me if you have any questions, and let me know how you are progressing.

Keeping You in the Game

Berry, Duthie & Miller

INTEROFFICE MEMORANDUM

To: Administrative Assistant

From: Director of Finance

Date: Today's Date

Subject: Budget

Attached is a template for a budget that I have edited by hand.

Can you please create a template for me to work with by next Wednesday; if you have any questions, please let me know. Thank you.

DRAFT BUDGET FORM   Project 3 – Task 2

COMPANY NAME

Budget
Month and Year

Trainers

Personnel	Budget	Actual	Difference ($)	Difference (%)
Office Staff				
Sales Staff				
Operating	**Budget**	**Actual**	**Difference ($)**	**Difference (%)**
Advertising				
Bad Debts				
~~Delivery Costs~~ *Fees*				
~~Dues and Subscriptions~~				
Employee Benefits				
Insurance				
Legal and Auditing				
Maintenance and Repairs				
Office Supplies				
Postage				
~~Rent~~ *Mortgage*				
Sales Expenses				
Supplies				
Telephone				
Utilities				
Total Expenses	**Budget**	**Actual**	**Difference ($)**	**Difference (%)**

Interest
Taxes
Shipping
Storage

Keeping You in the Game
Berry, Duthie & Miller

INTEROFFICE MEMORANDUM

To: Administrative Assistant

From: Director of Human Resources and Administration

Date: Today's Date

Subject: Requirements for New Office and Projections

As you know, Berry, Duthie & Miller is moving. Our planned date for occupancy is January 1, 20xx.

The following is the information for tables that I need prepared:

Staff Growth

- The column headings are year, no. of employees, increase, and projected number of employees.
- There are currently 50 employees, and this number will remain the same for 20xx.
- Calculate the projections for five years (20xx to 20xx).
- The projection is a 4 percent employee increase per year.

Office Space

- The column headings are year, no. of employees, increase, and square footage.
- Calculate the projections for five years (20xx to 20xx).
- The projection is 300 square feet per employee.

Lease Cost

- The column headings are year, lease cost, and increase.
- Calculate the projections for five years (20xx to 20xx).
- $160,000 for 20xx has been allocated.
- The projection is a cost increase of 3 percent annually.

INTEROFFICE MEMORANDUM FROM DIRECTOR OF HUMAN RESOURCES AND ADMINISTRATION Project 3 – Task 3 (Page 2)

Requirements Table

Following are the company requirements that I need put into a table in either MS Word or MS Excel:

- Occupancy Date (January 1, 20xx)
- Term (five-year minimum)
- Office Space (square footage per employee)
- Boardroom
- Kitchen
- Washroom Facilities
- Five Training Rooms (50-student capacity)
- Lease Cost
- First Right of Renewal Clause

Include a title and the corporate logo.

If you have any questions, please come and see me.

ROYAL REAL ESTATE

1339 Carling Avenue
Ottawa, ON K1Z 8N9

613-625-1291 (telephone)
613-725-3413 (fax)
www.royal.emp.ca

Today's Date

Mr. Jordan Runnalls
Director of Human Resources and Administration
Berry, Duthie & Miller
820 - 360 Albert Street
Ottawa, ON K1R 767

Dear Mr. Runnalls:

Subject: Office Relocation Options

Thank you for the opportunity of working with you on your new office relocation. Based on the requirements you have provided, the following are the three best options available for your timeframe.

Option A

18,000 square feet; $15,100 per month lease; five-year lease available January 1, 20xx; there is a first right of renewal clause available; two washrooms, one kitchen, one boardroom, space for six training rooms. The lease increase is 4 percent per year.

Option B

20,000 square feet; $14,000 per month lease for five years; 3.5 percent lease increase per year; availability is December 31, 20xx; first right of renewal clause in lease, one kitchen, space for five training facilities, two washrooms, and one boardroom.

Mr. Jordan Runnalls
Director of Human Resources and Administration
Today's Date
Page 2

Option C

18,000 square feet; $15,000 per month; six-year lease; 4 percent per year lease increase; available December 1, 20xx; lease to purchase, one kitchen, one boardroom, space for five training rooms, and four washrooms.

When you are ready to view these facilities, appointments can be arranged with 24-hour notice; in the meantime, I would be happy to answer any questions at your convenience.

Sincerely,

Myles Blair

Myles Blair

OFFICE RELOCATION PROPOSAL

YOUR NAME

DATE

——#— page break —#——

Table of Contents

Introduction . . . . page number

Requirements and Projections . . . . . page number

Options . . . . page number

Conclusions . . . . page number

Berry, Duthie & Miller is looking to lease an office space to accomodate it's projected growth over the next five years.

Fifty employees make up the staff of Berry, Duthie & Miller's new location. Projection is 4 percent per year determining that we will be housing 58 employees in 2018.

STAFF GROWTH TABLE

Square Footage of the office space must be a minimum of 17,600 based on 300 square feet per employee.

DRAFT REPORT   Project 3 – Task 9 (Page 3)

Berry, Duthie & Miller has projected a lease cost increase of 3 percent per year and is forecasting a funding of $180,081 for 2018.

Based on the three options for the new location, the projected lease costs for Options A, B, and C are:

1. Projection A:

2. Projection B:

3. Projection C:

After careful consideration, Berry, Duthie & Miller is choosing Option _____ as the new leased facility.

Fill in your choice of the best Option: A, B, or C

Notes:
Meeting to Plan the Annual Management Committee Meeting and Retreat

1. Theme for Retreat: The **Race** to Successs – **R**evenue, **A**ccountibility, **C**ustomer, **S**ervice **E**xcellence, **E**xecution.
2. Retreat arrangements:
    o Location – to be determined
    o Dates – Wednesday to Friday in the last week of March, 20xx
3. Guest speaker will be the chair of the local chamber of commerce – dir of marketing, sales to confirm by phone by the beginning of Feb
4. Social activities include a whine and cheese upon arrival on the first night and a kareokie party after the second evening's activities.
5. Transportation
    o Everyone to carpool; sign-up sheet to be distributed by Finance Dir.
    o Guest speaker may not be staying for entire event; he'll be driving himself

6. Menu Options –
will be available

> Everyone is to complete a form indicating meal perferences –
> Director of Finance to prepare and distribute by (you fill in a
> date)
> Everyone agreed that wine should be made available; this
> would be available at $5 per glass. A salad bar for lunch will
> also be offered at 3.25 per person

7. Room assignments – Rooms are double occupency. Sign-up
   sheets will be forwarded in advance by HR Director

8. Agenda items for the com'te meeting to be submitted by the

   second Monday in February.

Attendees:

Director of Finance (Acting Chairperson)
You (Secretary)
B. Bhatacharia
J. White
E. Drucker
P. Kyumoto
J. Spatula
R. Geddings
S. Neil
C. Crosby

Absent with regrets: D. Carver

Meeting called to order at 7:10 by the Director of Finance.

P. Kyumoto moved that the agenda be approved. S. Neil seconded the motion. The motion was approved.

A motion was made by J. Spatula that the last meeting Minutes be approved. B. Bhatacharia seconded the motion. The motion was approved.

Old Business

a) Telecommunications system – J. White advised that the telecommunications feasibility study would be completed by the end of the month. He will provide an update to board members at the next meeting.

Reports

a) Chief Executive's Report – The Director of Finance recommends that if a new facility is not found by the end of this month, the company should stay in the current location over the winter. A motion was made by E. Drucker and seconded by R. Geddings that the company remain in the same location. Motion approved.

b) Treasurer's Report – E. Drucker explained that a consultant, Susan Johns, reviewed the organization's bookkeeping procedures in preparation for the upcoming yearly financial audit. She found them to be satisfactory. E. Drucker reviewed highlights, trends, and issues from the balance sheet, income statement, and cash flow statement. Issues include high accounts receivables; these require Finance Committee attention to policies and procedures to ensure that our organization receives more payments on time. P. Kyumoto moved that the financial statements be accepted. J. White seconded the motion. The motion was approved.

c) Board Development Committee's Report – The Director of Finance reminded the board of the scheduled retreat coming up in March. Development Committee business will be discussed at the retreat. He will bring a copy of the draft agenda to the next board meeting.

d) Ground Committee Report – no report given.

DRAFT MINUTES (FORMAL STYLE)   Project 4 – Tasks 5 and 7 (Page 2)

The Director of Finance presented members with a draft of the reworded by-laws paragraph. The director suggested a resolution to change the by-laws accordingly. J. White will first seek legal counsel to verify that the proposed change is consistent with provincial regulations.

New Business

a) New hires – The Director of Finance announced the hiring of a new executive assistant, Lesley-Ann Lewinsky. She is scheduled to begin work at the end of the month. R. Geddings is to enrol Ms. Lewinsky in the company orientation program to be held the first week of March.

b) Information management systems plan – B. Bhatacharia noted that he was working with staff member Jacob Smith to help develop an information management systems plan. Two weeks ago B. Bhatacharia had mailed members three résumés from consultants to help with the plan. In the mailing, he asked members for their opinion to help select a consultant. The majority of members agreed on Lease-or-Buy Consultants. J. Spatula moved and E. Drucker seconded a motion to use Lease-or-Buy Consultants. The motion was approved.

c) Building renovations – C. Crosby reported that the property maintenance department has begun repairs on the roof. An area needs to be patched as a result of the ice storm last winter. The front entrance to the building will be closed for the next month until the job has been completed.

Next meeting – Last Wednesday in March

Adjournment – 8:45 p.m.

Keeping You in the Game

Berry, Duthie & Miller

INTEROFFICE MEMORANDUM

To: Administrative Assistant

From: Director of Training

Date: Today's Date

Subject: Annual Management Committee Meeting and Retreat

I would like you to begin planning the next Management Committee Meeting and Retreat to be held from Wednesday to Friday in the last week of March, 20xx. All directors should be in attendance as well as you, our Executive Assistant, Fiona Say, and our guest speaker, the chair of the local chamber of commerce. Please note that the chair is not able to stay for either evening and will be driving up early on the day of the speech.

The details for the event are as follows:

- The first day and last day will be allocated for transportation to and from the venue. However, an optional social activity is scheduled for the first night and breakfast will be provided on the morning of departure.
- Only the second day and night will have scheduled meeting activities.
- The venue should be a conference resort (i.e., one that provides meeting facilities and overnight accommodations). I would like you to investigate **one** option which should be within easy driving distance (i.e., no greater than 100 kilometres) from our office.
- Transportation to the venue should be by way of carpools with no more than three or four individuals to a car.
- A single room should be reserved for each participant.

Please research the following and provide me with an update on this research in memo format:

- The cost of the rooms, if available
- Services available at the venue for conferences
- Other services offered at the venue such as for dining and recreation

The draft agenda is attached. Please edit this and prepare an RFP for your selected venue. The agenda should be sent to the directors and the guest speaker. Include the driving directions and map.

Attachment

DRAFT AGENDA   Project 4 – Task 14

DRAFT AGENDA

<u>March xx</u>

7:30 p.m.	Dinner at _____ restaurant
9 p.m.	Wine and cheese in the lobby

<u>March xx</u>

7:30 a.m.	Breakfast
9 a.m.	Opening Remarks (Director of Training)
9:15 a.m.	Icebreaker
9:30 a.m.	Guest Speaker (chair, local chamber of commerce – "Innovation in the Workplace – an Urban Experience")
10:30 – 10:45 a.m.	Break
10:45 a.m.	Update on the new information management system (Director of Finance)
Noon	Lunch
1:30 p.m.	Brainstorming session on employee retention
3:30 – 3:45 p.m.	Break
3:45 p.m.	Workshop on sales techniques for front line sales personnel
4:30 p.m.	Free time
7:30 p.m.	Dinner at _____ restaurant

<u>March xx</u>

7:30 a.m.	Breakfast
9 a.m.	Departure

Diversified Events
Hong Kong

2104-5, 21/F, Island Place Tower • Island Place, 510 King's Road • North Point • Hong Kong • +852 3105 3970

February xx, 20xx

Mr. Blake Moore
Director, Marketing and Sales
Berry, Duthie & Miller
820 – 360 Albert Street
Ottawa, ON K1R 7X7

Dear Mr. Moore:

SUBJECT: Retail Hong Kong Expo

Andress Event Planners Inc. is pleased to invite you to the most important event for 20xx in the retail industry. Retail Hong Kong Expo, which will be held from Wednesday through to Friday in the last week of June, 20xx, will host over 4,500 top executives from some of the largest retailers, brand owners, and interior designers. This event takes place at the Hong Kong Convention and Exhibition Centre, which is located in the heart of one of the most exciting cities in the world.

The Retail Technology Expo will include exhibitors from some of the leading retail technology product and service providers. They'll be showcasing innovations in categories including labelling, cash management, and electronic pay solutions. The Retail Marketing Expo will feature exhibitors who focus on all aspects of shop design and visual marketing.

As well as the hundreds of ideas that you'll glean from the halls of our two exhibitions, there will be two seminar theatres dedicated to sessions that will guarantee to inspire and educate you. Thomas Reilly will return to discuss the practical applications of retail branding and Emmett Lee will discuss the importance of security applications in retail. These are just a few of our stimulating offerings for this year.

Enclosed is our brochure and registration form. This year's conference fee is 1395 HKD payable by cheque. Alternatively, you can pay by credit card by completing our online registration form found at our website. The official hotel, the Grand Hyatt Hong Kong, is directly connected to the convention centre. This beautiful hotel boasts eight world-class restaurants and a full complement of recreational facilities, including an award-winning spa. An information package will be mailed to you as soon as we receive your registration information. When reserving, please quote the conference identification number, RHKE. Your confirmation is required by the last Friday in March, 20xx.

Regardless of the economic climate, Asia's retail market has always been buoyant with an amazing potential for growth. You'll have the opportunity to benefit from the wealth of knowledge and technical expertise our exhibitors have to offer and to meet and do business with the key decision makers and influencers of Asia. Don't hesitate to contact me for more information. Hong Kong awaits!

Sincerely,

Jim Sugarman

Jim Sugarman
Sales Director

Enclosures (2)

Appendix G

Key Documents

KEY DOCUMENTS

The following files have been made available electronically to complete the tasks within the workbook (www.emp.ca/adminassistant):

Organization Chart

Logo

Templates

- Fax Cover
- Interoffice Memorandum
- Letterhead
- Request for Proposal
- Travel Authorization
- Travel Expense Claim
- Voice Message

Project Tasks

- Project 1 – Task 10 – Biography Voice File
- Project 1 – Task 13 – Draft Speech
- Project 4 – Tasks 10 to 17 – Interoffice Memorandum from Director of Training
- Project 4 – Task 18 – Teleconferencing PowerPoint Presentation
- Project 6 – Task 1 – International Travel Arrangements Research Table
- Project 6 – Task 10 – Passport Table

Pop Tasks

- Project 2 – Pop Task 6 – Voice Message
- Project 3 – Pop Task 12 – Voice Messages 1, 2, and 3
- Project 4 – Pop Task 19 – Voice Message